THE DALES WAY
and ACCOMMODATION GUIDE

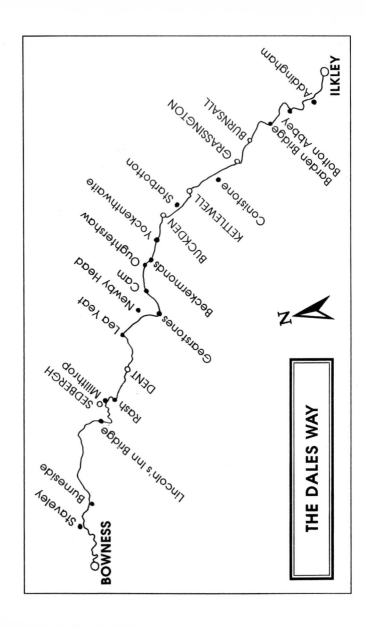

THE DALES WAY

BOWNESS
Staveley
Burneside
Lincoln's Inn bridge
Millthrop
SEDBERGH
Rash
DENT
Lea Yeat
Newby Head
Cam
Gearstones
Oughtershaw
Beckermonds
Yockenthwaite
BUCKDEN
Starbotton
KETTLEWELL
Conistone
GRASSINGTON
BURNSALL
Barden bridge
Bolton Abbey
Addingham
ILKLEY

N

THE DALES WAY
and ACCOMMODATION GUIDE

by

TERRY MARSH

CICERONE PRESS
MILNTHORPE, CUMBRIA

© Terry Marsh 1992

ISBN 1 85284 102 8

British Cataloguing-in-Publication Data. A catalogue record for this book is available from the British Library.

ACKNOWLEDGEMENTS
As ever I am immensely grateful to a team of friends and relations who made my task an easy and pleasurable one - my wife, Gaynor, and my father, both of whom completed the Dales Way in each direction, and repeated some of the sections, without a word of complaint.

Parents-in-law and our children tagged along from time to time. Dennis and Jan covered quite a bit of it with us, and helped with transport links, as did Jan's parents. Ron, a voluntary warden in the Yorkshire Dales National Park, and Jumbo, the biggest little dog ever to climb a mountain, respectively made sure I didn't cut any corners and inspected all the trees. Without their constant support and encouragement when I was having an off-day, their patience and understanding as they stood waiting in pouring rain as I made notes or muttered into my recorder, and their philosophical resignation as I pratted about taking photographs, I simply could not have completed the book either as quickly or as thoroughly as I did. To all of them I owe a debt of gratitude.

Sheila Roberts in the Yorkshire Dales National Park office gave helpful information on footpath changes, while the information sent my way by Carol Greenwood in Bradford's Libraries and Information Service was much appreciated, and all used. To the owner of the Old Rectory, Addingham, I am much obliged for information about his wildfowl collection, and for permission to mention it in the book. And finally, to the staff at the Reception, York Minster, I am obliged for your information and best wishes.

Also by Terry Marsh
 The Summits of Snowdonia
 The Mountains of Wales
 The Lake Mountains: Volumes 1 and 2
 The Pennine Mountains
 100 Walks in the French Pyrenees

Front Cover: Walkers on Top Mere Road between Kettlewell and Buckden

CONTENTS

Kilnsey Crag

INTRODUCTION

Beside the river we sat, munching pork pies and cold bacon butties, a steaming mug of coffee adding warmth to the smug sense of satisfaction we all felt. Back home it had rained hard during the night and on into day; should we or shouldn't we? We did, and only a couple of hours later, ensnared in rucsac's warm embrace, bade farewell to the solitary mallard at Ilkley's old bridge and set off for Windermere. Quickly we settled into that comfortable, easy stride of the laden backpacker, careful where we put our feet, early banter punctuated by the darting 'beep' of a dipper and the insistent calling of a cuckoo from deep within a thicket. The lazy murmur of the river, banks soft-moulded by time and water, hazy shimmer of bluebell fields, heady scent of honeysuckle, and across the scene drifted the thin sound of church bells striking the hour. Soon we would be on our way again, hour on hour easing along, serenaded by Nature's pastoral symphony; wet clouds drifting on the lightest of breezes, rays of sunlight probing their defences, stabbing at weaknesses to add sharp-edged colour to the day. Suddenly, mid stride we paused in unison, a curlew's bubbling trill drifted from the hillsides; no one spoke, a cloak of contentment folded its mantle around us; nothing jarred; we were at peace.

They seemed so long ago, those Elysian fields beside the Wharfe, scene of that privileged union with Nature. Yet in our memories they were only yesterday, and the day before, and the day before.

The Dales Way

Now well established among the hierarchy of Britain's medium distance footpaths, the Dales Way, like its big brother the Pennine Way, is a walk designed by walkers with walkers in mind. And for that reason alone it deserves our attention.

The Dales Way is very much a monument to cooperation between the Countryside Commission and the West Riding Group of the Ramblers' Association, and is officially recognised as a 'Recreational Path', a sort of Second Division National Trail, though eminently worthy of promotion. With commendable vision it was this arm of the RA that in the late 1960s foresaw the unquestionable appeal of a fine line through the valleys of the Dales and across the watershed of Britain into Cumbria, finally dropping to an abrupt end on the shores of the country's largest lake, Windermere. By pressing on to Windermere the originators of the Way effectively, and most attractively, linked two of the country's major national parks.

Most of the walk is along legitimate rights of way, but where gaps occurred the Way has been provided with alternative loops to make a continuous path. As time has gone on, many of those loops have been sanctified and become a part, albeit a 'permissive' part, of the Way itself. In a few nooks and crannies short stretches of the Way have had to be diverted, for a variety of reasons, and this guide encompasses diversions as recent as August 1991.

The nature of the countryside through which the Dales Way passes is such that this is a far less demanding walk than other middle- and long-distance paths, and for that reason alone ideally suited to walkers wanting either to complete the walk in sections, returning weekend after weekend until the whole route is covered, or those who want to tackle a multiple day walk for the first time. That is not to say the Dales Way is any kind of soft option, adverse weather while crossing between Cam Houses and Dentdale, for example, would test the most experienced walkers. But you are seldom far from help or shelter, while the discomforts and privations one generally associates with long backpacking trips are unlikely to prove a burden for long.

There is no question but that over the years of the Dales Way's existence it has significantly helped the local economies along its length, and many hitherto isolated farmhouses will now gladly furnish walkers with a range of facilities. But we must never forget that without the sturdy and friendly people who make their living from this often harsh environment there would be no Way. They are generous and tolerant to the extreme, but at all times we must respect their property and their privacy, especially at times of the year critical to the welfare of the farming economy. In particular take great care during lambing time between March and May (sometimes a little earlier), when dogs must be under the tightest of controls. From May into summer many of the seemingly lush meadows, alongside the rivers in particular, provide a vital hay crop for the hillfarmer. Where the Way goes through such fields, make a point of travelling in single file to avoid damage, it may be grass to us, but it is part of a livelihood to the farmer. Towards the end of the year, from mid-August, we have the grouse-shooting season, and while this will trouble walkers very little there are stretches where shooting does take place, on the flanks of Blea Moor, for example, and here great care is needed.

One of the great attractions of the Dales Way is that it is rarely far from features of architectural, social, ecological or historic interest - churches, bridges, manor houses, shooting lodges, Roman roads, ancient stone circles, packhorse bridges, suspension bridges, motorway bridges, viaducts, nature trails - the Dales Way has them all. It is, too, rich in flora and fauna, unbelievably so, and walkers intending to tackle the Way in one go would do well to allow time each day to take everything in. The interest never lets up, from the first step to the last. This surely is the hallmark of the greatest of walks, and in the case of the Dales Way a fitting testimony to the skill and vision of the men and women who pioneered its route. It is, too, a walk for all seasons, though spring and autumn have the edge, while with careful planning a winter walk is not beyond the bounds of reason and certain to add a whole new perspective to the landscape.

Go in peace, with an open mind, and experience the richness of our countryside the Dales' way.

EXPLANATORY NOTES
Distances
To ensure accuracy when giving distances, detailed measurements have been made using a Romer on maps to a scale of 1:25 000, where necessary measuring at 100-metre intervals. This produces an accuracy to within 25 metres per kilometre. At its worst extreme this would give a total distance for the Dales Way of 3 kilometres (1.9 miles) greater or lesser than the given overall distance; the probability, however, is that these minor variations cancel themselves out since they invariably arise where the Way meanders rather than follows a more direct line. It is not considered that such lack of precision will cause undue distress to walkers accustomed to regular outings over mountain terrain.

Using the Guide

The main route description is given in **bold** lettering in the text, while general comments are in normal type. The author's comments, observations, and general background information are given in *italics*. These occur in the text in the order in which they are encountered along the Way.

Where variant routes are given, these are indented and have a continuous black line running down the left edge of the page.

No attempt has been made to construct 'day length' sections, that is for the individual walker, but as a rule each short stretch ends at a location where accommodation, of one sort or another, may be found. (See also "Planning the Walk".)

PLANNING THE WALK

Having a number of long distance walks under my belt I know full well the importance of maintaining daily progress, of not falling behind schedule, especially if time is limited. But I know, too, that too much progress focuses the mind rather more on the end of the walk and not on what there is to enjoy throughout it. Keeping going, sticking to 14, 16, 18 miles each day, simply becomes a route march, and if you apply those tactics to the Dales Way you will be back home in no time wondering what all the fuss was about, largely having missed the point.

With so much of interest concentrated in so (comparatively) short a walk it is vital for full enjoyment to allow time to explore and potter about, to paddle in the streams and rivers, to visit churches (and pubs), to get something of a feel for the lifestyle that permeates the course of the Way and of the history that has fashioned the land it traverses. Generally, it is not a bad idea to take your cue from the rivers you will follow; nowhere do they charge headlong, save for the odd moment of madness, preferring to meander gently, switching this way and that to inspect nooks and crannies, going with the flow. You should do the same.

If time is limited then the Way can be completed comfortably in 6 days, stopping overnight at Burnsall, Buckden, Dent Head, Sedbergh, Burneside and Bowness. This will give an average daily walk of 22.5 kilometres (14 miles), quite a comfortable proposition for walkers accustomed to long distance undertakings. But those attempting a long walk for the first time (and the Dales Way is in that respect an ideal introduction) would be well advised to increase the number of days allotted for the walk. Better to sit at the end of a each day enjoying the afternoon sunshine and a quiet drink, than stomping on doggedly, grim-faced and determined, to find yourself searching for accommodation, pitching tents or cooking meals in gathering darkness.

To avoid imposing any set pattern on the walk beyond that demanded by the disposition of accommodation, no attempt has been made to configure the guide into daily sections. Each of the sections simply represents a linking together of two or more places that provide accommodation in some shape or form; the only exception to this rule is at Mill Bridge, Dentdale, a mere 2 kilometres (1.25 miles) from Dent itself. Given this format the walker can construct his or her own daily dosage, according to respective standards of fitness and competence, and inclination to wander and explore.

All of this pre-supposes walkers want to do the whole thing from end to end in the one endeavour, but the Dales Way also lends itself very much to completion on a piecemeal basis. There are generally good public transport services along much of its length, notably in the early and later stages, to facilitate walks that must return to base, while only a modicum of cooperation is all that is needed for groups of walkers with at least two cars to devise linear excursions. Public transport is also available at each end of the Way, both Ilkley and Bowness being convenient for British Rail links, the former from Bradford and Leeds, the latter by way of Windermere to Oxenholme on the Lancaster-Carlisle line.

Finally, one of the nice things about the Dales Way and the people who live and work along it is that you will often find, especially in the more remote sections, that proprietors will gladly run walkers to the nearest pub/restaurant, or meet them on the Way itself. Those proprietors who have mentioned this useful helping hand are identified in the Accommodation Guide which accompanies this guide. It should not be assumed, however, that others will not follow suit, so be forward enough to ask: the importance of making the day's walk suit you cannot be underestimated.

MAPS

The maps reproduced in this guide are based on Ordnance Survey maps with the permission of the Controller of Her Majesty's Stationery Office [Crown Copyright]. It is not intended that these should be a substitute for the use of conventional maps; they are provided for guidance only.

The associated use of Ordnance Survey maps will only enhance your enjoyment of the Dales Way, identifying features outside the scope of the maps in this book. The following maps will be needed:-

EITHER 1:50 000 Landranger Series
Sheet 97 - Kendal and Morecambe
Sheet 98 - Wensleydale and Upper Wharfedale
Sheet 104 - Leeds, Bradford and Harrogate

OR a combination of 1:25 000 Outdoor Leisure Maps and Pathfinder Maps
OLM 2 - Yorkshire Dales, Western area
OLM 7 - English Lakes, South Eastern area
OLM 10 - Yorkshire Dales, Southern area
OLM 30 - Yorkshire Dales, Northern and Central areas
Pathfinder 617 - Sedbergh and Baugh Fell
Pathfinder 662 - Bolton Abbey and Blubberhouses
Pathfinder 671 - Keighley and Ilkley

USEFUL ADDRESSES

Cumbria Tourist Board, Ashleigh, Windermere, Cumbria, LA23 2AQ (05394 44444)

Ilkley Tourist Information, Station Road, Ilkley, West Yorkshire, LS29 8HA (0943 602319)

Lake District National Park, Brockhole, Windermere, Cumbria, LA23 1LJ (05394 46601)

Rambler's Association, 1/5 Wandsworth Road, London, SW8 2XX (071 582 6878)

Yorkshire Dales National Park, Colvend, Hebden Road, Grassington, Skipton, North Yorkshire, BD23 5LB (0756 752748)

Youth Hostels Association, Trevelyan House, St Albans, Hertfordshire, AL1 2DY (0727 55215)

Friends of the Lake District, Kendal Road, Staveley, Kendal, Cumbria, LA8 9LP

Yorkshire Dales Society, 152 Main Street, Addingham, Ilkley, West Yorkshire, LS29 0LY

FACILITIES ALONG THE WAY

Accommodation

   Bed and Breakfast, Youth Hostels

      see 'Accommodation Guide'

   Camp sites

      Barden, Appletreewick, Threshfield, Kettlewell, Buckden, Cowgill, Dent, Sedbergh, Lincoln's Inn Bridge, Crook (see 'Accommodation Guide' for details)

   Bunkhouse Barns

      Barden Tower, Hubberholme, Oughtershaw, Catholes (see 'Accommodation Guide' for details)

   Inns

      Ilkley, Addingham, Bolton Bridge, Appletreewick, Burnsall, Hebden, Linton, Grassington, Kettlewell, Starbotton, Buckden, Hubberholme, Cowgill, Dent, Sedbergh, Kendal, Burneside, Staveley, Bowness

Railway service

   Ilkley, Cowgill, Kendal, Burneside, Staveley, (Windermere)

Post Offices

   Ilkley, Addingham, Bolton Abbey, Appletreewick, Burnsall, Hebden, Linton, Grassington, Conistone, Kettlwell, Buckden, Dent, Sedbergh, Grayrigg, Kendal, Burneside, Staveley, Bowness

Public conveniences

   Ilkley, Addingham, Bolton Abbey, Cavendish Pavilion, Burnsall, Hebden, Linton, Grassington, Kettlewell, Buckden, Dent, Sedbergh, Kendal, Burneside, Staveley, Bowness

Telephones

   Ilkley, Addingham, Bolton Bridge, Bolton Abbey, Barden, Howgill, Appletreewick, Burnsall, Hebden, Linton, Grassington, Conistone, Kettlewell, Starbotton, Buckden, Oughtershaw, Cowgill, Dent, Sedbergh, Lowgill, Grayrigg, Oakbank, Kendal, Burneside, Bowston, Cowen Head, Staveley, Bowness

ACCOMMODATION

The Dales Way is amply furnished with inexpensive bed and breakfast accommodation throughout its length, only becoming thin on the ground between Langstrothdale and Dentdale. So that Wayfarers may always have a ready and up-to-date listing of bed and breakfast facilities an "Accommodation Guide", detailing over 150 locations is given at the end of the book. It is intended that this guide should be updated annually. If any Wayfarers find other accommodation worthy of inclusion in the guide, please write to the author c/o the publisher. The author would also welcome information on properties found unworthy of inclusion, giving details, so that these may be removed from the list.

Not all the accommodation listed is immediately adjacent the Dales Way, and so some attempt has been made to identify approximate locations on the maps accompanying the Accommodation Guide. Wayfarers are advised to check the precise situation of intended accommodation halts in relationship to the Way before making reservations. Many proprietors will arrange to meet Wayfarers, and offer a 'ferry' service both to and from accommodation and places where meals may be obtained. Not all those listed have made this clear (a situation we hope to put right in future editions of the Accommodation Guide), so do not be afraid to ask.

EQUIPMENT

All walkers have their own preferences (and idiosyncrasies) in the matter of equipment and clothing. When extending day-walking into multiple day-walking much the same items are needed, but some thought needs to be given to matters of personal comfort in the hygiene department.

The following list may be found a useful reminder - rucsac (comfortable and well padded), boots, socks (and spare socks), trousers (or shorts, etc.), underclothes, shirt, midwear (eg. pullover) and spare, wind- waterproof jacket and overtrousers, hat, gloves, maps, compass, torch (with spare battery and bulbs), whistle, first-aid kit, survival bag or blanket, food and drink, insect repellent, ablution tackle, including half a roll of toilet tissue (for emergencies), small hand towel. Campers will also need such additional weighty items as tent, sleeping bag, Karrimat, cooking equipment and utensils.

Pedal bin-liners will be found useful for keeping wet clothing separate from dry, in the rucsac, and for containing rubbish until a suitable disposal point is reached.

Why not take a small notebook, and keep a daily log? Or a book to read in the evenings?

The old bridge at Ilkley, which marks the start of the Dales Way

THE DALES WAY

The romantic ruins of Bolton Priory on the banks of the Wharfe.
The remains of Barden Tower, once a hunting lodge.

Walkers on the banks of the Wharfe near Barden. (W.Unsworth)
Burnsall Bridge.

1. Wharfedale

ILKLEY

As a brief overture to the Dales Way, a tour of Ilkley would not be out of place. The whole of the Way is beauty (in all its guises) heaped upon beauty, and Ilkley a more than fitting introduction, probably unsurpassed as a setting off point for any of this country's major walks. It lies near enough to major towns and cities to be easily accessible, and provides a range of accommodation to suit all pockets.

Dominated by the brown dome of Ilkley Moor with which it is synonymous, Ilkley is an attractive town, bright and bubbling, a mecca for walkers from far and wide. Not surprisingly it has a considerable history as an important centre since Bronze Age times. It was known to the Romans as Olicana, but has also variously been known as Olecanon, Illicleia, Hilleclaia, Illelaya, Illeclat, Illeclay, Yelleilaia, Yelkeley and Hekeley. Before the Romans came, the land around Ilkley was occupied by the Brigantes, the ancient Celtic tribe whose great kingdom extended roughly to the boundaries of present-day Yorkshire. The Romans built a great fort here, and the lines of their roads can still be traced across the surrounding moors, indeed many of them will be encountered along the Way.

Under the Anglo-Saxons Ilkley became a manor, held for a while by the Archbishop of York, and later passed through various ownerships, serving time as a seat of justice for the great hunting Forests of Yorkshire. The manor rolls from the twelfth to the seventeenth century still survive and provide interesting reading. One record provides that "No tenant shall receive or harbour vaccabund or arrogant lyers but which are known to be borne within this wapentake..." Presumably, then, arrogant Yorkshire liars are OK, while arrogant Lancashire liars are not! Nor, the record goes on, are you permitted to house "evell condicioned women...", a circumstance that defies comment!

By the early eighteenth century Ilkley had degenerated into "a very mean place...dirty and insignificant...chiefly famous for a cold well, which has done very remarkable cures in scrofulous cases by bathing, and in drinking of it". Even so, Ilkley's fame as a 'modest' inland spa brought a *wealth that replaced medieval streets and cottages with more spacious houses and thoroughfares. Today it is a source of much interest for the historian and rambler alike, and a springboard for a host of fine walks, of which the Dales Way is but one.*

✳ ✳ ✳

An ancient Chinese proverb relates that a journey of a thousand miles begins with the first step. Likewise the Dales Way, though considerably less than a thousand miles will ensue, unless the wanderlust gains a hold and the Way is followed by the Cumbrian Way, the Southern Upland Way, the West Highland Way...well, you get my drift. How easy it is to set off from a humdrum everyday existence, and with that very first step, laden with so much promise, hope and aspirations, embark on a journey that might as well be a thousand miles or more, for does not that first step symbolise a crossing from one world to another, the start of an adventure, if only for a couple of weeks?

So, laden and prepared, we begin, the opening day barely leaving the riverside, except to avoid a dangerous stretch of road. The surroundings are quite agreeable, and in spite of the understandable reluctance to leave the Wharfe, remarkably varied and full of interest.

ILKLEY to BOLTON ABBEY
10.2 kilometres (6.25 miles)

Officially, the Dales Way begins at the Old Bridge, formerly a packhorse bridge, over the Wharfe (113482), built in the 1670s to replace a previous bridge washed away on a number of occasions by the river.

From the centre of Ilkley the Old Bridge is reached by heading down New Brook Street from the traffic lights near the parish church, and then through the riverside park, keeping on the south bank of the river until the Old Bridge is reached. By the side of the bridge a signpost unceremoniously marks the start of your journey with a fib, suggesting that the length of the Way is a mere 73 miles (117 kilometres) when in fact (as described in this book) it measures 78 miles (125 kilometres).

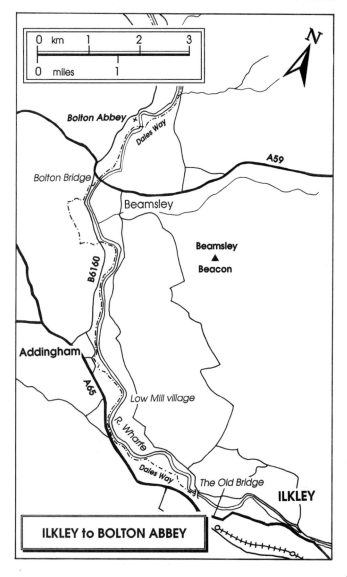

ILKLEY to BOLTON ABBEY

Without crossing the bridge head upstream along a tarmac track beside a nursery. This almost immediately brings you on to a footpath along the riverbank, and then as the river sweeps widely away the path gives on to a minor road leading to Ilkley's tennis club. Head towards the club buildings and on reaching them bear left at a public footpath sign and descend slightly to pass through a dilapidated kissing gate. A path across a field now heads away to another gate at the end of a short wall in mid-pasture. In recent times the gate has tended to be bypassed, though only (and unacceptably) at the expense of an adjoining wire fence. Future Wayfarers might therefore anticipate the restoration of the fence.

Beyond the gate the path follows the edge of the field to a kissing gate (signposted: "Dales Way") and continues across another field to a gate between two small trees. Press on ahead and follow the field to its far end and bear slightly left to a white gate. Go through the gate and continue ahead towards the river, still a little distance away. When the river is finally rejoined, near a building, an old kissing gate leads on to a narrow path, over a small footbridge, and on along the true right bank of the river sandwiched between the river and a fence.

The small wooded hillock along the edge of which the route travels affords charming glimpses of riverside scenes, a feature of much of this first stage of the walk, and one that characterises virtually the whole of the Dales Way.

The path runs through low scrub and bracken, damp in places, before climbing gently to pass a large white house on the left. Cross a feeder stream by a bridge and soon descend awkwardly as the path combines rocks and tree roots (slippery in wet conditions) to trip the unwary. Level ground follows and another feeder stream just too wide to jump when it flows after rain necessitates a slight deviation (left, or right through undergrowth - a simple footbridge would be a great help here).

Ilkley's golf course on the opposite bank eases into view, tempting for those who enjoy the game, but out of reach, and anyway this is much too early for diversions.

A pleasant stroll beside the river ensues and finally brings the Way to the old Addingham road, now a quiet back road parallel with the modern A65 trunk road. Use the old road as it follows the river until we are able to turn right into Old Lane (signposted: "Dales Way"), leading to Smithy Greaves and Holme Ings, part of a small housing estate.

*This is **Low Mill village**, now a peaceful retreat of carefully refurbished Industrial Revolution cottages won from the converted ruins of an old mill on the banks of the Wharfe. Amazingly, the mill seems to have survived the attention of the **Luddites**, an organisation of men, formed together in 1811, in a period of great distress, and opposed to the mechanisation of the textile mills in the industrial centres of the East Midlands, Cheshire, Lancashire and Yorkshire, believing it to be a cause of unemployment. In a five year period of wanton destruction they smashed machinery and destroyed the mills that housed them. The first outbreak was in Nottingham, and said to have been inspired by a young apprentice, Ned Ludd. By comparison with what followed that first upsurge was a token gesture, leading as it did to far more serious and organised rioting, especially here in West Yorkshire, where many people were killed, mills and machinery destroyed and rioters tried and executed or transported. Charlotte Brontë's novel,* Shirley, *is set in this troubled time.*

Nearby Addingham received its share of their rioting, but Low Mill seems to have escaped, and now presents an historically interesting interlude early in the walk.

Odd as it feels, we pass through the village to emerge at the far end by a small flight of steps on to a broad, metalled track heading for Addingham. In a short while the Old Rectory is reached, and its gardens and wildfowl collection bring an appropriate moment for a breather.

*The collection was originally started in the mid-1980s to give interest to the grounds surrounding the **Old Rectory**, and contains a wide variety of ducks - mandarin, pintail, teal, Carolina, muscovy and tufted - as well as Lady Amherst, Silver, Golden and Reeves pheasants. But the most stunning member of this select group is the albino peacock, against which its blue brethren paradoxically pale in comparison. These complement the geese - barnacle, Canada, greylag and common white - which arrived of their own accord.*

21

Described by their owner as "a modest collection where all the birds roam quite freely, and give pleasure not merely to [himself] but also village people and local walkers."

Rest a short while, but recognise, please, that the grounds are entirely private. The birds can easily be fed and viewed from the lower reaches of Low Mill Lane and the packhorse bridge, shortly to be encountered, where the public footpath crosses from Low Mill Lane to the church.

Continue along Low Mill Lane to turn right down a flight of steps to the old packhorse bridge, the "parishioners'" route to the church, and turn left across the ensuing field, keeping the church on the right, to intersect the footpath to the church.

Addingham Church is one of a few in this region to possess blue-faced clocks - along the Dales Way another will be encountered in Dent. This is a 'fashion' started by the old established clock-making firm of William Potts and Sons of Leeds, with work on Bradford Cathedral, since when the firm has been asked to paint the dial on several clocks. The blue paint is specially mixed and is known as "Potts Blue", it having been found that numerals in gold leaf are even more legible on a blue background than on black or any other colour.

Follow the path away from the church to meet the access road to its car park, and in a short while leave it, right, for a narrow ginnel (and bridge) between cottages, leading on to North Street. Turn right and continue slightly uphill into Bark Lane.

Addingham is a neat village, now thankfully bypassed on the A65 by the heavy traffic which used to shake its very foundations. The village grew largely during the Industrial Revolution, but its greatest claim to fame is that it sheltered Archbishop Wulfhere of York (from AD854 to 900) who fled here when the Vikings began their campaign of terror against Christian people, first crossing the Humber and bloodily capturing York in AD867.

Just after a left bend, take a descending path (signposted), right. Ignore the modern suspension bridge to Beamsley, but continue upstream down a few cobbled steps to rejoin the river. When the path forks, take the lower route to the right, back to the

riverbank, and press on through a gap in a wall with another small mill redevelopment, High Mill, for a moment deflecting the route away from the river.

Another minute and the entrance to a caravan site is reached. Enter the site and follow the main road until at a signpost the Way is routed back to the edge of the river. Keep along the bank to a step stile, where the bank is quite sandy. Follow the river ahead on a green path.

Continue along the bank unfailingly upstream, crossing a succession of stiles, until the path once more forks (less noticeably) just after a stile. Either way is feasible, though the lower soon diverts you steeply up a slope to gain the higher, left, path, which reaches the same point less demandingly.

Close by, a derelict barn, now sprouting well established trees from its interior, tells of former, less mechanised times when the transporting of fodder and farmstock was a time- and energy-consuming business best avoided, if possible. Barns such as this, many of which will be encountered along the Way, would have seen active service in years gone by, housing hay stocks, and sheep at lambing time.

Shortly the Way is forced, rather pointlessly (for the want of another stile) on to the B6160, quite a busy little thoroughfare to be encountered again before long. On this occasion only a few strides are necessary to leave it abruptly at a stile onto a footpath trekking around the perimeter of a field.

This fairly new footpath is vital to the welfare of Dales Wayfarers in that it avoids a nasty stretch of roadwalking, but the first section is narrow, at the top of an embankment above the Wharfe, and fringed on the left by barbed wire fencing.

From a stile the path descends a steep flight of wooden steps to regain the level, riverside ground of Low Park.

*Low Park was once part of the parkland around Farfield Hall, and from this stretch of the river there are splendid views to the wooded hillside of **Beamsley Beacon**, which commands the surrounding countryside as a beacon should, having been used in medieval times to signal events across the north of England as part of a chain of bonfires.*

Keeping faith with the river the path eventually finds itself forced into a small copse of rhododendron, sycamore and beech before emerging by steps and a stone stile on to the B6160 once more.

Officially now the Dales Way turns right to follow the road, but quite frankly, having experienced it, this is during summer months a risky proposition. There is no footpath along the road, and heavily laden walkers are compelled to quarrel as best they might with oncoming traffic along a road that twists and turns as it descends towards Bolton Bridge. Go this way if you must, taking great care if you wish to reach Bowness, until, as the road levels and with Bolton Bridge in sight, a narrow, low gap stile on the right gives access to roadside meadowland and a narrow footbridge across a feeder stream.

As a better and infinitely safer option, turn left along the B6160 for a short distance, and then right (signposted: "PF") for Farfield Farm. Walk up the farm access track, staying on the main track, left, when it forks. Go right to pass stables and on through the farmyard, keeping ahead between open barns and cattle sheds. Shortly pass between some old railway abutments, and turn right to follow a broad track to a gate giving on to open hillside pasture.

Approaching Bolton Bridge, along the Wharfe

Now climb diagonally left aiming for the top edge of Eller Carr Wood, which can be seen in the distance. A stone "through" stile helps you cross a dry stone wall, and once over it, follow the top edge of the wood, keeping to a narrow path more or less parallel with a wall, and about 25 metres (yards) from it.

There is a splendid panorama over this section of the valley and of the distant summits of Earl Seat, Simon's Seat, and Beamsley Beacon, which more than justifies (if justification is needed) the scant effort required to tramp up here. It is, too, the first real opportunity to get above the valley, to feel the refreshing openness of this remarkable landscape, to get a glimpse of things to come.

By following the wall another, at right angles, is eventually reached, where a stile lets you into Lob Wood at the top of a steep slope. Go right, along a wall, until the path turns left, and descends rather precariously on a narrow, shaly and slippery path to pass beneath the arches of the former railway line. Continue ahead and then right on a leafy path, shortly descending left to reach the B6160 at a narrow and slightly obscured gap. Cross and follow the road for approximately 250 metres (yards) to the gap in the low wall on the right mentioned earlier.

Cross the footbridge and follow the right hand edge of a pasture to reach the cottage by the side of Bolton Bridge. Pass through a gate, and climb steps to gain the bridge, cross the road, go through a gate on the opposite side into wide pastures flanking the Wharfe, and simply follow the river to the increasingly impressive edifice of Bolton Abbey (shops, café, toilets through the "Hole in the Wall" at the top of a broad flight of steps on the left, well before the abbey is reached).

Follow the riverbank to a bridge spanning the river.

BOLTON PRIORY (BOLTON ABBEY)

*Around 1154 a small group of Augustinian canons, led by Prior Reynald, came to this heavily wooded stretch of the Wharfe from Embsay, where conditions had become "unfavourable", to make a new start. The land was endowed by **Lady Alice de Romille (or Rumilly)** of Skipton Castle, for "the wellbeing of my soul and those of my forebears and descendants". It is indisputably a magnificent setting of meadows and woodland that once would have sheltered wolves, the windswept moors and fells rising*

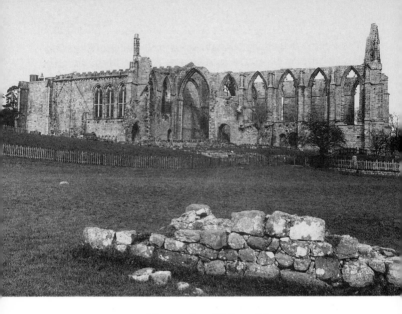

The remains of Bolton Abbey

majestically all around. Not surprisingly the Priory (often also referred to, less correctly, as Bolton Abbey) attracted the attention of poets, painters and writers like Turner, Cox, Girtin, Landseer, Ruskin and Wordsworth.

The Augustinians were popular residents, ordained priests living together like monks, but very much involved with the local people. Their unremitting round of duty, prayer and worship, seven times a day, seven days a week, invariably had them rising at 2am to begin their devotions. But it would be rendering them a disservice to portray this community's existence as one exclusively of meditation and the seclusion of cloistered life. A vastly different picture of medieval life, both monastic and agricultural, survives in the household book of Bolton Priory (the **'Compotus'**), compiled between 1290 and 1325, and, according to antiquarian Dr T.D. Whitaker, "a folio of a thousand pages, very fairly written [in a] kind of patois, consisting of Byzantine Greek, Italian, old French, and Latinised English". From it we learn that this Augustinian house, its 15 or so canons supplemented by lay brothers and gentlemen retainers, was also home to a motley crew of serfs and free servants, raising its resident population to almost 200.

Life was a busy, boisterous affair, much consumed with the practicalities of everyday life. Bolton Priory managed mills and granges far and wide, and extra help at harvest time ran to over 1000 haymakers at a wage of two pence a day. The Priory worked a lead mine, collected tolls from Embsay Fair, ran a forge, a shepherd's lodge at Malham, and another at Nussay on the edge of Knaresborough Forest. There were cooks, carpenters, herdsmen, smiths, bakers and brewers, all documented in the Computus, even to their rustic names, Adam the Stockman, Whirle the Carter, Botchcollock the Cowper, Simon Paunche, Adam Blunder, Tom Noght and Richard Drunken. So great, in fact, was this communal 'flock' that their collective annual appetites alone accounted for 64 oxen, 35 cows, a steer, 140 sheep, 69 pigs, large quantities of wheaten bread and oatmeal pottage, the malting of 636 quarters of oats for ale, and 1800 gallons of wine. By all accounts the Priory oven was so big that, after the Dissolution, it sheltered a flock of 60 sheep.

Clearly, the Augustinians had moved a long way from their vow of poverty. Nor did the monastic vow of obedience attract much closer observance: one William de Appelton, caught poaching, refused to reform, despite a penance which included scourging, confinement to the Priory, and a simple fare of bread, beer and vegetables on Fridays. Another lay brother, contrary to the rule of poverty, hid his life's savings of 100 shillings, while another, "taking delight in debates and envyings, constantly stirs up strifes, quarrels, and backbitings among his brethren".

Then, suddenly, in 1539, all was threatened with total obliteration under Henry VIII's wholesale destruction of the monasteries. Work on the building was abandoned, the canons dispersed, lead torn from the roofs, furnishings stripped out, and the greater part of the estate sold to the Clifford family, later to pass to the Cavendishes, Dukes of Devonshire. Fortunately, the nave was secured intact, and today, restored and re-restored (as recently as 1982-5), it sees service as the Priory Church of St Mary and St Cuthbert.

These days we see tourists, weekenders and Dales Wayfarers where black-robed canons and their retainers once strolled, but otherwise it would be easy to roll back the years; a few buildings are gone, but so much remains unchanged. For most walkers it is too short a day to halt at Bolton Priory, but it deserves at least an hour of your time, and comes at a spot when an hour's break is perfectly in order before pressing on.

❋ ❋ ❋

BOLTON ABBEY to BARDEN BRIDGE
5.5 kilometres (3.25 miles)

Cross the footbridge at Bolton and turn left on to a large open pasture for our first taste of the Wharfe's true left (eastern) bank, which surprisingly is not dissimilar to its true right bank! Immediately to hand (or perhaps, to foot, would be more appropriate) a track rises, right, by a flight of steps to continue as a broad footpath steadily climbing above the Wharfe. Eventually this joins the minor road, Hazelwood Lane, near Pickles Beck. The same point is reached by taking a lower and initially less obvious path from Bolton footbridge, skirting the pasture (and thus short-cutting a loop in the Wharfe), against the eye-catching backdrop of Lord's Seat, and crossing a stile to reach wooded river slopes. The path undulates a bit before climbing in easy stages to meet the higher path.

Cross Pickles Beck by a ford, and turn immediately left on a footpath heading back towards the river, to another signposted path going right through a gap stile and on to a broad path leading unerringly to the bridge at Cavendish Pavilion.

Tea and snacks are generally available at Cavendish Pavilion throughout most of the year, and with so much attractive scenery, pleasant circular walks, nature trails and an abundance of nearby parking, is inevitably a honeypot that on fine weekends swarms with visitors quite like nowhere else along the Way until you reach Bowness.

Between Bolton Abbey and Barden Bridge prominent footpaths travel both banks of the river, and it matters not which side is preferred. From Cavendish Pavilion there is some suggestion that the official line takes the path on the left bank (east), but Ordnance Survey and other maps denote its line along the right bank, passing through Strid Wood in which the Bolton Estate has devised a number of Nature Trails. The Strid Wood option is preferred here.

Cross the bridge to Cavendish Pavilion and turn right heading across a small car park to the entrance to Strid Wood.

A small shop here sells a variety of maps, booklets, sweets, etc., and used to levy a small toll for entering the woods, which are private, and its pathways permissive only. The toll no longer applies (though there is no guarantee it will not return!)

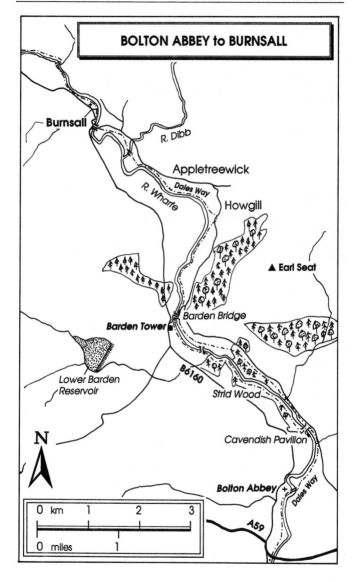

*The bridge at Cavendish Pavilion. From here the Way
enters Strid Wood*

STRID WOOD

You don't have to be a trained naturalist to recognise immediately that
Strid Wood is somewhere quite special, and almost certainly unique. It will
be a rare occasion if you have the wood to yourself for its heavily-laden
beauty and powerful natural qualities draw people from far and near to
potter about among moss-covered grottos, banks of fern, trees, rock
formations and cascading water. Magnificent at all times of the year, it is
exceptional in spring and autumn, the one when the myriad wild flowers
that colonise this narrow sanctum are bursting through, the other when the
burnished bronze colours are at their most intense.

Not surprisingly in 1985 the wood was designated a Site of Special
Scientific Interest (SSSI) under the terms of a management agreement
with the Nature Conservancy Council, for it contains the largest area of
acidic oak woodland and the best remnant of oak wood pasture in the
Yorkshire Dales National Park.

But it is the chasm of The Strid itself that is the greatest attraction. Here the river, intense, agitated, laden with the waters of a score of mountains, squeezes itself through a narrow channel between the rocks, setting up forces that have claimed many a life. Indeed legend has it that it was the drowning of Alice de Romille's son, the **Boy of Egremond**, in the early part of the twelfth century that caused his sorrowing mother to found the first priory of Augustinian canons that in 1154 was to become Bolton Priory. Alas, this is an easy legend to dispute since the lad's signature appears on the deed of endowment of the land on which the priory now stands. Nevertheless, it is a powerfully dangerous spot, and no place for a quick dip, however much you might need it.

At one time the river of The Strid would have flowed in a small waterfall or rapids over the outcrop of rock lower downstream. To begin with the erosion of the softer rocks would have formed a series of potholes which in time linked to produce a deep chasm and underwater system. The danger lies in its great depth, not quite so obvious when viewed from above, and the sheer force of water. In 1984 a group of sub-aqua divers from Leeds University carried out an underwater survey, in spite of great difficulty in standing against the strong current and flow of debris. Although they were unable to reach the base of the main waterfall, its depth was calculated at thirty feet.

Strid Wood is renowned for its wealth of flora and fauna. Most of the trees are broadleaved, either sycamore or beech, the larger of which are between 250 and 300 years old. In addition there are about 10% ash, 6% birch and a small number of oak. The ornithologist will discover as many as 62 species of nesting bird, while naturalists interested in lichen will find Strid Wood to be unrivalled in Yorkshire, with over 80 species, twice as many as elsewhere. Other surveys list 97 species of fungi, 40 of mollusca, 41 of liverworts, and 98 mosses, many rare or very local in distribution: altogether a remarkable place.

❋ ❋ ❋

As you enter Strid Wood follow the broad track ahead, and basically keep going. There are a number of colour-coded trails (originally laid out in the 19th century by the vicar of Bolton); the one we want is green. Continue following this trail, ignoring deviations left and right, until you reach an information board close by The Strid. A short diversion is necessary to inspect The Strid proper.

Barden Bridge

Continue upriver, this time making use of the yellow trail, which climbs along a ledge to a spot high above the river. After a while the path descends again to rejoin the river before it bends left and climbs once more. At a junction follow the path ahead, staying with the river by means of a neatly arched modern footbridge, finally leaving Strid Wood at a stile and gate. Easy grassy embankments lead to an old aqueduct carrying Nidderdale waters to Bradford taps. Cross the aqueduct and continue on the left bank, always close by the river, to Barden Bridge. [The author has a slight preference for passing beneath the aqueduct and remaining on the right bank as far as Barden Bridge, on the grounds that it provides a better view of the river sweeping away to Barden Bridge. Just before leaving the woodland which gathers close by Barden Bridge on the true right bank, a metal notice indicates that the woodland was substantially replanted in 1894 - which gives some idea of what 100-year old trees look like.]

Barden Bridge is a delightful monument in itself, narrow and not at all suited to modern traffic, while its neat pedestrian alcoves offer a

Linton Church, near Grassington. (W.Unsworth)

Kettlewell from Top Mere Road

splendid vantage point looking east to Earl Seat and west to Barden Moor.

BARDEN TOWER

A short deviation from the Way is needed to visit Barden Tower, though one of the buildings in its grounds has been converted to provide bunkhouse accommodation, and as such is most useful to Dales Wayfarers, especially since the former priest's house nearby is now a small restaurant and serves afternoon teas.

In its early days Barden Tower was just another hunting lodge, but it grew in stature when the feudal baron at Skipton, one of the Clifford line, for four centuries lords of Skipton and Craven, decided to furnish it with a comfortable bed for the night. As he would always travel with a retinue of hangers-on something more spacious was needed.

Now the Tower is a ruin, as it has been for almost 200 years. Once it was a formidable construction, built very much with marauding Scots in mind, though there is no evidence that its defences were ever put to the test.

✳ ✳ ✳

BARDEN BRIDGE to BURNSALL
5.8 kilometres (3.6 miles)

After the gentle pasture by which the Way came finally to Barden Bridge (1676), the route continues with the true left bank and presses on past a roadside parking area to squeeze between a wall and the river. Much of the path is criss-crossed by tree roots, making progress a little awkward, and a better proposition is simply to follow the path from the relative safety of the adjoining roadway; it is only a short distance anyway to a signpost ("Howgill: 1m") marking the path's return to the riverbank and the start of an easy-to-follow stretch courting the sparkling river closely.

Wide open views expand ahead, with Barden Moor and the wooded slopes of Earl Seat remaining prominent. Many of the steep-sided and overhanging riverbanks serve as accommodation for nesting sand martins

Left: The River Wharfe at New House Farm, Langstrothdale

in season, while the river is patrolled by mallard, dippers, grey wagtails and the occasional goosander.

As Howgill, as yet unseen, is approached, a line of stepping stones across the river tempt a short diversion, and a short way further the path swings away to cross the inflowing Fir Beck.

Howgill, not quite on the Way, remains a short distance away along a lane, and has a few tea rooms, a camp site and a shop. It is a scattered community nestling at the base of Simon's Seat, and in 1310 was the site of one of six hunting lodges comprising the ancient Chase of Barden. Now it is the gateway to Skyreholme valley, the limestone gorge of Trollers Gill and the house and grounds of Parcevall Hall, to which a short excursion, if time permits, is well worthwhile.

Parcevall Hall was built in the seventeenth century, but has much of an Elizabethan look about it, and for those who marvel still at the craftsmanship of this country's ancient masons a wonder to behold. The landscaped terraces, too, are quite splendid, and the woodlands and rock gardens, rather like Ingleborough Hall near Clapham, host a fine collection of rare and exotic plants from many parts of the world.

Cross the bridge over Fir Beck and immediately turn left to regain the river by a path (signposted: "Appletreewick" and "Burnsall"). Continue with the path sandwiched between Haugh Wood and the river, with nothing to lead us away from what is delightful scenery, until Woodhouse Farm intervenes. En route, just after leaving Haugh Wood, a level meadow offers an agreeable camp site on the riverbank, though there are no facilities, and a notice at Appletreewick saying 'No Camping', though camping does take place. During summer months the meadow is used as a car park. At the far end of the meadow a track leads up to Appletreewick, where refreshments may be obtained.

APPLETREEWICK

Appletreewick for its size has more than its share of claims to fame, though most visitors find its name fascinating. Once, but no longer so I have been told, it was known colloquially as 'Ap'trick', and was a village of some importance in medieval times. Of Norse origins, it is recorded in the

Mock Beggar Hall, Appletreewick

Domesday Book as being owned by the English thanes Dolfin and Orme.

Clinging to the flanks of Kail Hill, Appletreewick is a one street village, but few come better than this. Fine old buildings line the street on both sides, climbing from Low Hall, past Mock Beggar Hall halfway up the street to High Hall, not surprisingly at the top.

High Hall *has a minstrel gallery in its main room where musicians would perch to provide the Baroque equivalent of background music, and only a little imagination is needed to tease the thin-noted strains of Thomas Tallis, William Byrd, Dowland and others from the strongly silent walls.*

Mock Beggar Hall*, originally Monk's Hall, housed the monks in charge of Bolton Priory's property hereabouts, and is the smallest of the three halls, but most certainly the oldest. Outside a flight of stone steps lead to an attractive old door and doorway, more than likely the stairway to someone's bedroom.*

They used to grow fine onions in Appletreewick, and Onion Lane testifies to the fact, but it is the story of ***William Craven****, born here in a cottage in 1548 (now part of St John's Church), hallmarked by the generous and loyal service he gave to his beloved Wharfedale, that inspires one more* *telling. Around 1562 William was sent to London by carrier's cart to be bound apprentice to a merchant tailor. By the time he was 21 he was a member of the Merchant Taylors' Guild, and in due course entered into business at a great mansion house in Watling Street. He became increasingly successful and popular, and in 1594 gave the enormous sum of £50 towards the building of St John's College, Oxford. In 1600 he was elected Alderman for Bishopgate, and a year later was chosen Sheriff of London. His success continuing he was knighted by James I in 1603, the year of his succession to the throne, and in 1611 became Lord Mayor of London. Could the authors, I wonder, of a popular Christmas pantomime satisfy a claim that "The characters and situations in this pantomime are entirely imaginary and bear no relation to any real person or actual happenings?", or was the cat introduced simply to protect the innocent?*

*On a less well authenticated note hangs another tale, of a giant hound named the **Barguest** or "**Mauthe Dog**". Spectral hounds haunt every corner of Britain, indeed one will be encountered further along the Way at Cam Houses, but the Barguest was real enough to those who encountered it. Fortified by the comfort of twentieth-century realism such legends have a hollow ring, but the tale's survival hints at something lurking in our subconscious. While from fairly recent times comes the story of a youthful motor cyclist chased to Appletreewick from Skyreholme by a huge, fierce-looking dog. On reaching Appletreewick the hound disappeared down a side lane, yet locals assured him no such lane had existed at that place for at least 100 years! It is not known what became of the youth, but an encounter with the Barguest usually meant death.*

✳ ✳ ✳

The Way now continues with the river until channelled through Woodhouse Farm.

*Woodhouse, a seventeenth century manor house was once the home of an almost forgotten Wharfedale poet, **John Atkinson Bland**. Styled as the "Wordsworth of Wharfedale", Bland was a picturesque figure, and left a lasting impression of a cultured, kindly old gentleman, proud of Bonnie Burnsa' and the long lineage of Dalesmen which he represented.*

He was, in his day, the best known man in Wharfedale, and very much a champion of Wharfedale's causes, great and small. His letters to the Skipton press were endless, but as they were invariably anonymous people

The Wharfe, near Woodhouse Manor

were left guessing as to their origin until another writer gave a clue away by observing: "It was with a **bland** smile I read, etc. etc."

Continue straight ahead beyond Woodhouse Farm to a narrow footbridge, and on across a field.

Close by rises Kail Hill, geologically one of many reef knolls around Burnsall, rounded green hills of pure limestone lying along the North Craven Fault, and formed as the land to the south slowly subsided.

When Burnsall finally appears ahead a beeline may be made for the start of the bridge, beyond which the village is entered.

BURNSALL

Many consider, with a lot of justification, that Burnsall, squatting comfortably beneath the gritstone moors of Burnsall and Thorpe Fells, is all that a Dales village should be, with its meandering river, five-arched bridge, a village green, inn, church and Tudor grammar school with diamond-paned windows. The picture is beautiful from every angle, the easy contours of the hills, their slopes covered with pine and beech, purple-hazed heather and bracken, everything just as it should be. It is

37

Burnsall

almost certainly of Norman origin for its name means 'Bjorn's Hall'.

There has been a bridge across the Wharfe at Burnsall certainly from the thirteenth century, with rebuilding in 1612 under the benefaction of Sir William Craven, and on into the nineteenth century.

But once more it is Craven's generosity that provides perhaps the finest building in Burnsall, the grammar school, now the village primary school. Founded in 1603 as a free grammar school for poor boys, and endowed by Craven with £120 a year for a master and £10 for an usher, it continued as a grammar school until 1876 when it became Mr Stead's School, with several boarders notably from Leeds and Bradford.

The church however owns a more ancient past; it has an evocative lych gate, its font bears pagan Norse symbols, and it contains carved Viking tombstones in the form of a 'hog's back', but were meant to represent a Danish house, carved with tiles and with a dragon's head at their ends. Now we are returning a thousand years into the church's past, and still encounter old memories enshrined in the dedication to St Wilfrid who was Abbot at Ripon in 671.

Another inscription reads: "This church was repaired and butified at the only costes and charges of Sir Wm Craven knight & alderman of the cyttye of London, & late Lord maior of the same, anno Domini 1612." Not content with that, Craven "did cause all the church & chancel to be furnished with stalles and seates of waynscote", walled the churchyard and constructed a "causey" from his birthplace at Appletreewick to the church.

❋ ❋ ❋

BURNSALL to GRASSINGTON
5.5 kilometres (3.4 miles)

As if wanting to distance itself from the tumult and clammer that is Burnsall on a fine weekend, the Way hastens to regain the banks of the Wharfe as soon as Burnsall Bridge is crossed, descending immediately right and following a good path behind attractive cottages and houses.

Not surprisingly the stretch of the Way leading away from Burnsall is

Loup Scar

39

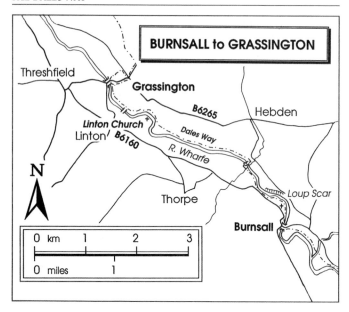

immensely popular, for every new twist in its trail springs into view an aspect, a new angle that quite simply is delightful, and no more so than when the cliffs and rapids of **Loup Scar** are reached. Here the Wharfe seems to delight in its own extravagant beauty as it flows through the limestone fault that created the Scar.

The scene of beauty now, but in 1766 Loup Scar was the spot where **Tom Lee**, a violent and hot-tempered Grassington resident with a less than affable reputation, tried to dispose of the body of a local Doctor Petty whom he had murdered for no more apparent reason than the doctor's telling him to mend his drunken ways. Described, though with uncertain foundation in fact, as the local blacksmith, Lee was a sometime leadminer and landlord of the Blue Anchor Inn. Bearing an easily aroused hatred, Lee lay in waiting for the doctor, and as the physician went home from the Kilnsey inn where he had admonished Lee, he was sprung upon and beaten to the ground at the north end of **Grass Wood**.

With a doggedness that has a commendable and persistent, if these days unacceptable, sense of justice about it, Lee, to whom all suspicion pointed (one version relates how he was seen disposing of the body by two lovers), *was twice tried and twice found not guilty. Unfortunately, when still not quite sober, he had made the mistake of boasting about his handiwork, so making his young apprentice, Jack Sharp (be it blacksmith, leadminer or publican is no longer clear), accessory to the murder. As Sharp grew older and more troubled of conscience he told all he knew to an avowed enemy of Lee's and turned King's Evidence. The third trial found Lee guilty, and he was hanged at the entrance to Grass Wood where he had committed the crime. Today, the flower shop in the village centre occupies the site of "Lee's smithy".*

The path to Loup Scar arrives eventually at a gate above the gorge from where it descends to wander pleasantly through woodland to a suspension bridge (025624) spanning a normally calm stretch of the river below Hebden village. Constructed by public subscription during the last century to replace stepping stones just downstream, the bridge is a speedy crossing of the river, but not one with stout people or heavily laden backpackers in mind for they might well need a push to pass across its waltzing span.

Once across the bridge turn left through a stone stile and continue along the north bank of the Wharfe down an avenue of trees, chestnut, beech and oak, designed it seems with the peaceful plod of Dales Wayfarers in mind. The Way emerges from this sheltered environ to see the Wharfe set off in a loop, a minor deviation avoided by heading across pastureland (footbridge midway) to reach a gate and stile leading on to a broad access road serving nearby, but screened, sewage works.

Directly ahead, across the Wharfe and reached by stepping stones, stands **Linton Church, St Michael's and All Angels,** *surely one of the most individual of Dales churches. Not unlike Bolton Priory, Linton Church occupies a bend in the river, though Linton is much nearer the water and its churchyard actually clinging to the riverbank - should ever the river find new force and contrive to undermine the churchyard, one of the strangest Armadas ever seen might well be found sailing down the river.*

Linton Church is old, very old, and of quite unique construction, squat and without a tower. It dates from the twelfth century, possibly during the period of church building that characterised Henry II's reign (1154-89), and is certainly different from any angle. Of course, the church we see today

41

is much altered and enlarged, especially during the fourteenth century, from the simple structure it would have been in its original days, but at least it still retains a chancel arch and two bays of the north aisle that are thought to date from about 1135 (which would place it earlier than Henry II's reign, in the time of King Stephen).

Adventurous souls might want to follow the footsteps of the ancient parishioners and cross the Wharfe here by the stepping stones, rejoining the Way at Linton Falls footbridge, but this is not the safest of propositions, and quite impossible unless the river is exceptionally low. The wisest course is to follow the access road for a while and at a bend cross a stile leading on to a path, left (signposted), heading back to the Wharfe's company opposite Linton Church.

Soon, with only the odd stile or two hindering progress, the route arrives at Linton Falls, where a growth of new houses has sprung up on the site of an old mill.

Linton Mill was built by J. and W. Birkbeck in 1790, though there is evidence of a mill on the site as early as 1258. The mill, which had five storeys and ceased textile production in the 1950s, was destroyed by fire in 1912 and later rebuilt only to be finally demolished in 1983.

Nearby, grooved by the feet of countless mill lassies and churchgoers, is Little Emily's Bridge, a small packhorse bridge on the original church path from Threshfield, which dates from the fourteenth century. It is thought to have been named after a member of the Norton family, who took refuge nearby at the time of the Civil War. Others suggest it may have been the invention of historian and novelist Halliwell Sutcliffe, whose works during the early years of this century - The Striding Dales, Through Sorrows' Gate, Ryecroft of Withens and Mistress Barbara Cunliffe - drew from the rich seam of life that peopled this region, and introduced many people to places they had never known or knew existed.

Linton village lies across the Wharfe, and has one of the parsimoniously few youth hostels along the Dales Way. A diversion to Linton, whether by adjusting the day's walking to use the youth hostel, or just out of curiosity, will be rewarded by rural charm at its most relaxing (weekends excepted, of course!), a place where life goes on much as it has done down the ages. In his book, Yorkshire Villages, Bernard Wood provides an anecdotal glimpse of Dales life, commenting that "A tourist once asked an old dales' villager, 'How on earth do you pass the time here in winter?' 'Well,' came the reply, 'we mak' up a good fire i' t' kitchen, an' then we all sit round and have a good laugh about t' queer folks who've been 'ere i' t' summer.'" And quite right, too!

Linton Falls are a tremendous spectacle, especially when rains have supplemented the river's normal flow; here the Wharfe argues with the North Craven Fault, tumbling angrily over limestone ledges to the quieter reaches beside Linton Church. A new bridge spans the river here and proves a fine vantage point. This is the fourth bridge to have occupied this site, the first, known as the Tin Bridge, was built in 1814 by the Birkbecks for their workers. It was covered by sheets of metal from old oil drums, and this was what gave it its name. A second bridge replaced the original in 1860, and a third in 1904. This became dangerous and was closed in 1988, being replaced by the present bridge in 1989 which is said to have a life expectancy of 150 years!...I wonder how they know?...and will anyone be around in the year 2139 who can get in touch with me to let me know if they were right?

Just by the bridge the Way crosses Sedber Lane, a direct route to Grassington. But continue ahead (not across the bridge) following the river, and just after a wall moving slightly away from it to reach an enclosed path beneath terraced houses leading to the main road at Grassington Bridge.

At the risk of stirring up confusion, Grassington Bridge was formerly known as Linton Bridge, which one might suppose to be a more appropriate name for the Tin Bridge. The original downstream section of the bridge was humpbacked and erected in 1603, then used by packhorses. Repairs and widening were carried out in 1661 and 1780, and the bridge raised to its present level in 1825. The cantilevered pedestrian footpath on the upstream side was added in 1984.

Go right now up the road into the centre of Grassington, though the Way actually crosses the road to a stile and follows a circuitous and wholly unnecessary loop into the village. The main street climbs easily, flanked by shops and hotels, cafés, guest houses and bed and breakfast places, making this is logical and convenient place to stay.

GRASSINGTON
Grassington has a fascinating history, as an important settlement during Iron Age times, with sites in Grass Wood and at Lea Green (until fairly

The village centre, Grassington

recently known as the "old Town") producing evidence of Brigantian settlement extending well into the Romano-British era. Now one of the best loved of Dales towns and villages, the town started to grow when the estate was transferred from the Percys to the Plumptons in the twelfth century, though the Angles must have built their huts here as long as thirteen centuries ago. Indeed, it was almost certainly the Angles who named the place, the "garrs" or enclosures they constructed leading easily into "Garrston"; "Grass Ings" also suggests a number of enclosures, many of which are still discernible.

The Plumptons held the manor of Grassington for 400 years until the male line died out and it was awarded, following a long legal contest, to one of the heirs female whose daughter married a Clifford.

During the seventeenth and eighteenth centuries the village's economic well-being developed notably as a result of leadmining and textile industries, for many years providing an important source of income. How extensive leadmining became may be deduced by just a cursory glance at the map covering Grassington Moor, where "Area of Disused Mines and Shafts" appears numerous times. Once the lead mines closed the village suffered a slow decline, but the prosperity that went was returned in increasing measure by the growth of tourism, enhanced by the opening in 1901 of the **Yorkshire Dales Railway** between Skipton and Grassington. And though the railway has now gone, tourism remains very much the mainstay of Grassington's economy today.

Long undisputed as the 'capital' of Upper Wharfedale, Grassington now hosts the offices of the **Yorkshire Dales National Park**, at Colvend, adjoining which is a National Park Information Centre.

✳ ✳ ✳

GRASSINGTON to KETTLEWELL
10.1 kilometres (6.25 miles)

Unable from Grassington to make much further progress along the Wharfe, at least once Grass Wood is reached, the Way is compelled to seek out an alternative but no less pleasant line, a high-level route, a moorland walk of considerable beauty and with views of distant purple hills and open moors. Alas, this deviation from the river's course can be confusing in misty conditions, and in bad weather should be shunned altogether in favour of a steady plod along Grass Wood Lane and the ensuing lane linking Conistone and Kettlewell. Such a foul weather alternative is not as bad as it seems, for it leads quickly to the water-shaped limestone of Ghaistrill's Strid, one of the loveliest stretches of the river, even on a bad day. If this option is needed, return to Grassington Bridge and regain the riverbank by a path, easily located, down a short lane on the east side of the bridge.

From Grassington Square head up the main street to the Town Hall with its splendid chestnut tree planted in 1887 to commemorate Queen Victoria's Golden Jubilee. Here, at a crossroads, turn left along Chapel Street, following this to the outskirts of the village. When the lane turns sharply left, leave it for a signposted path entering a farmyard on the right. This leads to a track through a farm gate after the last building. Continue beyond the gate, following a wall, to arrive at three gates in close proximity. Take the middle one, and cross the ensuing field to a narrow gap stile at the far end. Descend a little into the next pasture and

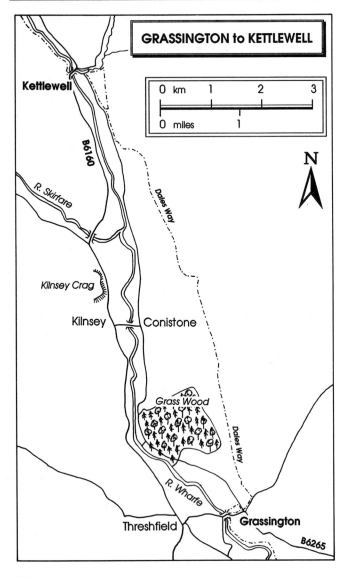

GRASSINGTON to KETTLEWELL

curve round, left, to another narrow stile in the far wall, cross the next enclosed field to yet another stile, this time giving open access to the broad expanse of Lea Green (997657).

Lea Green is the vast field system of an ancient British settlement, thought by scholars to be Iron Age, though sometimes bearing the description Romano-Celtic which generally suggests that the Romans found it already in working order and left the inhabitants to carry on with their farming.

Once on the edge of Lea Green a broad track is crossed, continuing ahead on a green track up a slight rise, ignore any paths going left. Soon a near parallel wall appears on the right and at a distance escorts the path through some low limestone outcrops until the two come together at a stile in the far corner of the field, with a dew pond close by the wall.

Cross the stile and the next field skirting well-defined limestone outcrops (left), and crossing a ruined wall to a gate on the left. Then pass a series of fields and stiles, en route encountering a rather substantial old lime kiln. Level pastures now precede an easy pull to the head of Conistone Dib, a great natural dry gorge descending steeply on the left. Ignore the stile near the top of Conistone Dib, and continue ahead across a bridge to enter a short enclosed way to a gate giving on to an old packhorse road, Scot Gate Lane.

Ignore Scot Gate Lane, and go straight ahead to a signpost pointing out a green track running beneath a limestone escarpment, Hill Castles Scar, on the right. Ahead now the eminence of Conistone Pie springs into view, a small knoll crowned by a large cairn, easily reached after the next stile.

Conistone Pie, boasting enough nooks and crannies to evade all but the most determined winds, is well worth a short break. Visible from many parts of the valley, this curious topknot from a distance resembles a man-made tower. Closer acquaintance however shows it to be a perfectly natural limestone sculpting. On a clear day the view is most commanding, reaching far up the valley to the vast expanse of Yockenthwaite Moor, while nearer to hand the vertical and overhanging cliffs of Kilnsey Crag seems like child's play at this safe distance. A little further right Littondale joins the main valley, with the long

47

The Way ahead: Wharfedale viewed from Conistone Pie

Birks Fell-Horse Head ridge rising invitingly between the two.

On leaving Conistone Pie the Way now proceeds along a level grass-covered limestone ledge above Swineber Scar, a spot with a curious attraction for heath snails. After a while the scar on the right that has accompanied the Way since Scot Gate Lane expires. From this point go straight ahead to a stile by a gate on Highgate Leys Lane at the edge of a small plantation of pine trees. Descend left through the gate on to a track that leads eventually to the back lane linking Conistone and Kettlewell.

Turn right along the lane, passing the entrance to Scargill House, since 1959 a Christian retreat and conference centre. After a couple of minor bends take a signposted path, right, leaving the road and continue to pass through a stile before the next gate. Now the Way follows a pleasant series of stiles and enclosures that lead to the edge of Kettlewell at a narrow green lane. Turn down the lane to a T-junction, and then right to emerge on a back lane. Now go left, pass the King's Head and then right to reach the main road through the village.

KETTLEWELL

Kettlewell is a tough abiding place, a delightful jumbled village that has withstood the passage of traffic of one sort or another for centuries. Thankfully, the main road only grazes the village, leaving much of the fine array of old lead miners' cottages that comprise a good part of Kettlewell unaffected. If there were more 'spokes' radiating from it, Kettlewell could accurately be described as the hub of upper Wharfedale, but there is only the main valley road, leading north to Starbotton and Buckden, and the former London to Richmond coaching highway struggling (in the end unsuccessfully) with the punishing gradient of Park Rash to the head of Coverdale. Even so, Kettlewell remains very much a focal point, and we see it today much as it has been for three or four centuries.

Kettlewell, an ancient community in a time-worn landscape of great beauty

There is some uncertainty, of no great importance, about the derivation of its name, some linking it with an Irish-Norse chieftain, Ketel. But the village undoubtedly pre-dates the Domesday clerks who came here in 1086 close to the end of their time limit. Sadly, they recorded little that might betray images of life in the Kettlewell of old. Later records prove more helpful, and make clear the importance of Kettlewell's position. From the head of Coverdale once came pedlars and packhorse men, along the route from Wensleydale and Scotland, making for Kettlewell's markets, though these suffered a decline after mass disafforestation in the early seventeenth century. Two centuries later sees Kettlewell thriving once more with inns, schools, bakers, cobblers, lead mining, cotton spinning and weaving.

Although the lands around Kettlewell were in the possession of a Norman baron we know that the sitting English tenants stayed put and persisted, as later charters with Anglo-Saxon signatories demonstrate. The Norman landowners later granted holdings in Kettlewell to Coverham Abbey and Fountains Abbey, which explains why Kettlewell church, like those at Burnsall and Linton, was of two medieties, ie. having two parsons, whom, one hopes, preached the same gospel in all things. In due course the manor of Kettlewell returned to the crown, and during the reign of Charles I found responsibility being passed to the City of London. The City of London, having little use for such distant outposts other than as staging posts on long distance highways, eventually sold the manor in 1656 to a group of yeomen, trustees for the freeholders of Kettlewell.

Sheltered on the north, east and west by high fells, Kettlewell, even in the depths of winter is noticeably warmer than many neighbouring villages, a place of peace and quiet where "limestone terraces, with the fringes of hazel and rowan coppices, give...a characteristic beauty". To some extent that is still true, but Kettlewell now is an immensely popular place, lying close by Great Whernside along a most attractive section of the dale. Rare it is at any time of year that the riverside pathways and the rising fells all around are not dotted with the brightly coloured clothing of walkers. The village is well able to satisfy the needs of Dales Wayfarers, having shops, good accommodation, a camp site, youth hostel and three inns.

✳ ✳ ✳

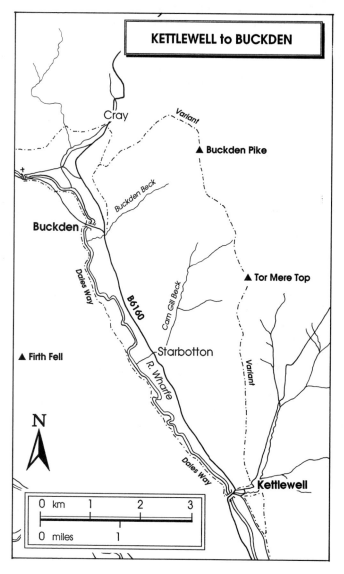

KETTLEWELL to BUCKDEN

Cray

Variant

▲ Buckden Pike

Buckden Beck

Buckden

Dales Way

B6160

Cam Gill Beck

▲ Tor Mere Top

▲ Firth Fell

Starbotton

R. Wharfe

Variant

N

Dales Way

Kettlewell

| 0 km | 1 | 2 | 3 |

| 0 miles | 1 |

KETTLEWELL to BUCKDEN
6.6 kilometres (4 miles)

Between Kettlewell and Buckden the Wharfe meanders through the wide glaciated valley bottom, frequently swinging about in extravagant loops and barely falling 25 metres (80 feet) throughout its length. With our river very much (as a rule) in relaxed mood along this stretch of the journey it is difficult to inject any pace into the day. And it would be an abuse of Nature's privilege to race by when all about you is saying: "Slow down, take it easy." If it's exercise you want, try the variant routes (described below), otherwise make the most of this last undemanding link before venturing into the wilder and ultimately more remote reaches of Langstrothdale. (Note: If you do intend to take the high level route over Buckden Pike and to continue via Cray and Scar House, bear in mind that Kettlewell will represent the last chance to stock up with supplies much before Dent, 47 kilometres (29 miles) away.)

Leave Kettlewell by going left along the B6160 to cross the bridge and turn immediately right through a gate. Follow the river's bend until, as it changes course again, we can pass through a gate (left) to follow the edge of a pasture to another gate letting us back to the riverbank.

Now all that is needed is to follow the Wharfe, usually a field or two away, on an excellent path - sometimes enclosed between walls, sometimes across open meadows, but always perfectly obvious - until Starbotton footbridge is reached.

A mere 3 kilometres (1.9 miles) separates Kettlewell and Starbotton along the Dales Way, and walkers preferring solitude may find Starbotton's welcome just a little more gentle than Kettlewell's. It isn't Kettlewell's fault, of course, it's just that Kettlewell is a focal point, Starbotton isn't.

STARBOTTON
Lying halfway between Kettlewell and Buckden, Starbotton is a compact collection of seventeenth- and eighteenth-century houses, many, especially the latter, smaller and neater, a legacy of the leadmining era when the surrounding hillsides were plundered for their hidden wealth.

Very much a place that one passes through rather than visits (a factor that could well be appreciated by its inhabitants), it is a wonder that

Starbotton has survived for so long without being consumed by the hills. It lies at the foot of Cam Gill Beck, many of its grey roofs sagging as if pressed upon by the weight of the hills, seemingly defenceless and at the mercy of the gill. Indeed, on more than one occasion the beck has attempted to engulf the hamlet, its most notable success in 1686 when in a few minutes a terrible storm turned the beck into a raging torrent, pouring down the hillside. One old record recounts: "the rain lasted 1½ hours, the hill on one side opening up, and casting up water to a prodigious height". The village, many of its houses but recently built, took the full force and was almost swept away; cottages were knocked down, while those that remained were filled with mud and water, and acres of fields covered with mud and stones.

The present day footbridge is close by the ancient crossing point for packhorse ways across the river, from Ribblesdale and Littondale in the west, via Walden Road to Wensleydale in the northeast, and via Starbotton Road to Coverdale in the east.

✳ ✳ ✳

From Starbotton footbridge the Way remains along the Wharfe's western bank, though the river soon leaves us once more. The path then heads on by a left-hand wall, occasionally enclosed, until the river is almost rejoined beneath Birks Wood. Now the path ascends slightly left from a gate (a little sketchily) to join a wide track. Soon after passing a barn head towards the river by dropping down to a gate in a wall, and from there simply follow the river's course to Buckden Bridge.

The village of Buckden lies a short distance up the road, to the right, and is the last opportunity to obtain supplies for quite some time. Walkers electing to follow the variant route via Buckden Rake, Cray and Scar House to Hubberholme or Yockenthwaite (described below), should turn right at the bridge for the village centre.

[The on-going description for the main line of the Dales Way continues on page 56.]

Variant: KETTLEWELL TO BUCKDEN VIA TOR MERE TOP AND BUCKDEN PIKE
Kettlewell to Buckden Pike summit: 7.5 kilometres (4.7 miles)
Buckden Pike summit to Buckden village: 3.5 kilometres (2.2 miles)

The Dales Way enters Kettlewell close by the bridge in front of the Bluebell Hotel (established in the seventeenth century).

Once fed and watered, or having passed the night in the village, cross the "Bluebell" bridge and turn right to follow the course of the beck for a short distance. Continue between houses to a road junction (post office on the right). Keep ahead on the minor road to Leyburn, and shortly turn left to tackle a 25% gradient (1 in 4 in old English!). The agony is only short-lived, for as the Leyburn road turns right, you must keep ahead on a broad track (signposted: "Cam Head"). This is Top Mere Road (shown but not named on the 1:50 000 map), and its ascent, a little stiff at first, soon eases as it rises steadfastly up the crest of the tongue of ground sandwiched between the Wharfe and Cam Gill (not to be confused with the Cam Gill which descends to Starbotton).

Eventually you break free from the constraining walls which have accompanied you thus far, and there is a fine sense of openness and freedom.

Away to your right the skyline is dominated by the long edge of Great Whernside, beyond which rises the River Nidd, and gradually the view opens up northwestwards to Yockenthwaite Moor and Langstrothdale.

The track shortly meets another old path, Starbotton Road, just beneath a small hummock. The Road leads you, left, to Starbotton (and is a convenient escape route should you need to return quickly to the main valley, though retracing your steps is a speedier way of getting back to Kettlewell), or, right, along Tor Dike to the head of Coverdale. By crossing the Road and ascending ahead a little you will find a stile at the rear of the hummock, and this marks your onward route. Cross the stile and you begin what on a tiring day can seem like an interminable ascent along the line of a wall, over an intermediate summit, Tor Mere Top, to Buckden Pike. There are some wet stretches near the wall in places, but nothing detracts from what in favourable conditions is an excellent and enjoyable walk, safe even in poor visibility, first to a small tarn near Tor Mere Top, and then on to a prominent memorial cross erected by a Polish airman, the lone survivor of a plane crash in 1942. From here it is an easy walk to the summit of Buckden Pike, with far-ranging views and a fine sense of achievement.

When the summit plateau is crowded with visitors who have dawdled up from Buckden, a diversion to gaze down on the vale of Walden, very much a secret valley, is always a good idea.

To reach the village of Buckden cross the stile on Buckden Pike's summit and descend, initially northwestwards and then southwestwards, along a good path to Rakes Wood and, ultimately, to Buckden.

Walkers not visiting Buckden, and intending to continue to Cray should resist the temptation of a beeline, but stick with the Buckden path until it joins the level upper section of Buckden Rake (941784), and then turn right, following the route described on pages 60-63.

BUCKDEN

There is a tang of wild places about Buckden, the 'valley of the bucks', and the home of deer as far as records take us. The settlement is a Norman foundation set up as headquarters of the Longstrothe hunting forest, and originally the creation of the Percys who held the land and set up ten hunting lodges at Cray, Chapel (Hubberholme), Kirkgill, Ramsgill (Raisgill), Yockenthwaite, Deepdale, Middlemore, Beckermonds, Oughtershaw and Greenfell (Greenfield). Once the hillsides echoed to the huntsman's horn, indeed deer roamed the wooded slopes of Birks Fell until as recently as the early 1950s, but, alas, there are none there now.

In former times Buckden was a bustling place, the 'last village in Wharfedale', boasting three inns. The 'Low Cock', in a yard opposite Buckden House, was the first to disappear, while the white house up a lane at the top end of the village was formerly the 'High Cock'; now but one, 'The Buck Inn', remains where long ago farmers came to sell their wool. Like an unpolished gem the village lies on a green- and bracken-coloured cushion in a fold of high hills, hemmed in by a beauty that makes the heart ache and the spirit rejoice.

Longstrothe Forest once spread from Buckden to the headwaters of the Wharfe on Cam Fell, though "Longstrothdale" as a geographical notion extended as far down-dale as Kettlewell. Quite why the name swopped its first "o" for an "a", is not clear, nor why only the stretch of the Wharfe between its birthplace and Buckden is now known as Langstrothdale, when the greater extent is well documented.

During the fourteenth century wolves were still hunted in Longstrothe Forest, an activity evidently supported by the religious houses, who were also the landowners, as the accounts of Bolton Abbey reveal, for among others they include the name of one W. de Hamleton, whose hunting forays would conclude their "sport" by visiting the Priory for "hospitality". Sceptics might wonder whether it was slain wolves or venison the hunters brought to the Priory tables, for the de Hamleton name, which first appeared in 1303, occurs with notable frequency.

✳ ✳ ✳

BUCKDEN to YOCKENTHWAITE
4.5 kilometres (2.7 miles)

The first objective beyond Buckden is the hamlet of Hubberholme, barely two kilometres down the road into Langstrothdale. Two possible routes present themselves; one, the true Dales Way, follows the valley, while the other, more demanding both of time and energy, and not for walkers wanting to make progress, scampers around the upper rim of the valley, visiting the ancient hamlet of Cray and Scar House, former Friends' Meeting House, before slowly descending to rejoin the valley route at Yockenthwaite.

On the one hand the variant walk (detailed on pages 60-63) has expansive, airy views of this far corner of Wharfedale, but misses Hubberholme, while the converse is true of the valley route. One way of resolving the issue is to extend your stay in or around Buckden to allow a circular walk using the variant walk as far as Yockenthwaite, returning along the valley with time to visit Hubberholme church.

Descend from the village on the minor road leading to Wharfe Bridge, and just after the bridge gain a broad path on the right (signposted: "Dales Way"), courting the river.

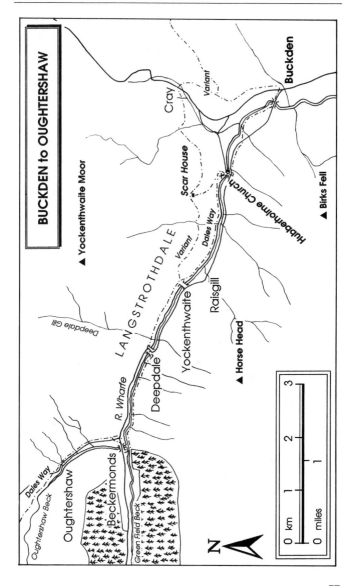

BUCKDEN to OUGHTERSHAW

Two hundred years ago, when the Wharfe Bridge was only half its present width, it was known locally as "Election Bridge", a nickname derived from a speech by a would-be Member of Parliament in which he promised to have a new bridge built if the local populace voted for him. This they did, but in the end a touch of eighteenth-century "virement" was introduced to divert funds from an existing allocation for the repair of Hubberholme Bridge.

Follow the path alongside the river; it maintains a level course throughout its brief but pleasant length before finally returning to the road for the short stretch to Hubberholme.

HUBBERHOLME

In the Domesday survey, Hubberholme, then recorded as "Huburgham", is noted as part of the manor of Kettlewell, though there is evidence further up the valley of an Iron or Bronze Age presence here, and in many ways it is easier to visualise prehistoric man stalking the wooded slopes than the hunting nobility of medieval times.

Though barely a hamlet (a "humlet", perhaps?), Hubberholme possesses two fine buildings both worthy of attention. Like a caring shepherd keeping watch over his scattered flocks, the venerable church of St Michael and All Angels is a real attraction, set among hills dressed in larch and fir, a timeworn place of worship still very much as its architect intended. Originally the church was used as a forest chapel, and in 1241 given to the Monks of Coverham Abbey by William de Percy, when it was known as the chapel of St Oswald of Huberham. It possesses various altars, one, a Jacobean altar originally at University College, Oxford. But its best feature is undoubtedly its oaken rood loft, one of only two remaining in Yorkshire, placed in the church in 1558, and one of the few to have survived the edicts of Elizabeth I that all such trappings should be destroyed. Outside the River Wharfe flows swiftly by, and once overflowed, carrying live fish into the nave of the church.

*Across Hubberholme Bridge stands **The George Inn,** a former landlord of which, also the Parish Clerk, coveted the oldest altar (now on the south side of the church) and had it removed to the inn as an ale bench, claiming, as Parish Clerk, an entitlement to put the altar where he wanted. Such secular misappropriation was inevitably frowned upon, and the landlord ordered to return the altar to its rightful place.*

*The George Inn, however, is still the venue for an annual "**land-***

Hubberholme Bridge

letting" ceremony held on the first Monday in the New Year (except when such a day is New Year's Day). This takes the form of an auction timed by candlelight, at which bids are made for a year's use of a pasture owned by the church. The last bid before the flame flickers out becomes the rent payable. Bids, made by the "Commons" in the bar, are considered by the "Lords" (the Vicar and his Churchwardens) in the parlour, and the rent of the successful bidder used for charitable purposes in the parish. By all accounts the ceremony becomes something of a merry occasion, in more ways than one: should you ever consider attending, be there early!

Very much a tranquil scene today, remote yet part of a widespread community, Hubberholme holds more than passing interest, and is likely to waylay Wayfarers' plans of a speedy passage up the valley. That it is indeed remote, especially in winter, is best summed up by the Reverend Miles Wilson, who in 1743 announced that his services at Hubberholme would be "once every Lord's Day in the afternoon, except in the winter quarter, when it is in the forenoon every other Sunday, because it is with *great danger and difficulty I pass over very high mountains and large drifts of snow to the chapel".*

✳ ✳ ✳

But now the heartlands of Langstrothdale await. Pass through a gate near the church, and once beyond the churchyard wall abandon the wide access track leading up to Scar House, to pursue a lower path (signposted) across meadowland and so regain the river.

Up-dale lie Yockenthwaite and Deepdale, similar farming hamlets that probably have altered little over the centuries since Langstrothdale Chase was a jealously guarded hunting haunt. As elsewhere, the Wharfe is a popular restaurant for feeding dippers, pied and grey wagtails, while the flanking trees and mossy walls offer an appetising à la carte menu for tree creepers, nuthatches, wheatears, pipits and the various members of the tit family.

The riverside path is nowhere in doubt, never straying from the river bank by more than a few metres, and soon reaches Yockenthwaite, where the path goes through a narrow gap in the wall just before the first gate giving access to muddy sheep enclosures, from which more gates and treacly conditions underfoot lead to a broad farm track. Move diagonally right and slightly uphill towards the main buildings, before pressing on to Deepdale.

[The on-going description for the main line of the Dales Way continues on page 64.]

Variant: BUCKDEN TO YOCKENTHWAITE VIA CRAY
6.5 kilometres (4 miles)

At the northern end of Buckden village follow a broad track that leaves the National Park car park, rising easily through Rakes Wood on the first stage of the ascent to Buckden Pike. This is Buckden Rake, a continuation of Gilbert Lane further north that goes over the Stake Pass into Raydale, on the line of the Roman road from Bainbridge to Ilkley.

As a gate is approached the angle of the rake eases, and soon a track deviates uphill towards higher ground and Buckden Pike. Ignore this and continue ahead along the level edge of a limestone escarpment. This brings you to a wall and gate with a narrow stile to its right. Squeeze through the stile and keep ahead for a short distance to a narrow gate where a footpath sign indicates a descent to Cray, a tiny hamlet now immediately below us.

With the benefit of height the whole of this magnificent limestone landscape is revealed, the high moorland plateaux and the deep trough of Langstrothdale with the infant Wharfe flowing casually through the centre of it, gathering steam.

CRAY

Cray is perched bravely on the steeply descending highway from Aysgarth in Wensleydale, what little space there is between the hillsides also shared with Cray Gill that here performs a series of miniature waterfalls amid banks thick in spring with violets, pansies and primroses. Not surprisingly, for the beck comes sparkling keenly from the moor, Cray takes its name from the beck, "crie" being a Middle Welsh word meaning 'fresh' or 'clean'.

The old inn at Cray, the White Lion, is widely renowned, and was the safe haven for that sole Polish survivor of the bomber crash on Buckden Pike in 1942. What a joy the White Lion must have seemed to him as he crawled from the hillside.

✳ ✳ ✳

From the gate on the edge of the escarpment the descent is initially steep (and slippery when wet) and leads beside a wall to a footpath sign and a short descent to a gate. Now Cray Gill is encountered, and crossed by a ford, to reach the road.

Pass behind the pub on a broad farm track (signposted: "Stubbing Bridge" and "Yockenthwaite"). Two tracks are encountered, the higher track proving to be the recommended route and leading to a gate (FP sign: "Scar House" and "Yockenthwaite"). From here the continuation is quite evident, keeping very much to the edge of the escarpment, and heading across the top of one of the incursions into the limestone edge to accommodate Crook Gill. Cross the gill by a bridge and keep ahead along a level grassy ledge.

Now, high above Todd's Wood, there is a splendid view down the length of Wharfedale to Kettlewell while across dale Buckden Pike displays its striated layers of rock, formed in an ancient sea and sculpted long ago by retreating glaciers.

The path closes in on a wall, and squeezes around its edge directly above Hubberholme, to continue rather less evenly than before, trending right to keep above the intake wall. Uneventfully, the call of curlew and golden plover on the air, we reach Scar House, once a prosperous place of worship, but now on the brink of dereliction.

*It was at **Scar House** in the seventeenth and eighteenth centuries, so defiantly near the old church of Hubberholme and its traditions, that there grew and flourished the new religion of the Quakers, largely inspired by **George Fox** whose vision on Pendle Hill of "a great people in white raiment by a river side, coming to the Lord" sent him scurrying about these northern parts - Wharfedale, Wensleydale and Westmorland - preaching the perfectibility of all men through inward personal experiences. More than once George Fox and the Quaker movement are encountered as the Way presses on into the remote landscapes of quiet farmsteads and high places from where came Fox's most ready converts.*

George Fox visited Scar House twice, first in 1652 when the resident James Tennant, "a solid yeoman", and his family were convinced, and then again in 1677. Between the visits James Tennant was fined for refusing to take the oath and was taken to York Castle where he died for his belief, an early sufferer for the Truth of the Quaker religion that was only to find acceptability with the passing of the Toleration Act in 1689.

It is not clear whether the Scar House we find today is substantially the same Scar House George Fox knew. A door-head bears the date 1698 and the initials I.A.T., while a second date, 1876, marks the time when the house was undoubtedly altered by Sir John Ramsden (of Buckden). Some accounts, however, suggest there was an intermediate house, three storeys high, one storey having been removed by Ramsden, but quite when or how this second phase of development occurred is now obscure.

Numerous rock steps enliven the course of the Wharfe

Pass round the back of Scar House and continue across limestone pavement to a gate and a gap stile in a wall. The looping path, less obvious now, continues along the southern fringes of Yockenthwaite Moor, to the hamlet of the same name, approaching which it has been diverted along a higher course to meet a broad, graded access track leading down to the valley.

En route the path passes, not that you would notice it, the fissured entrance to **Strans Gill Pot***, a cave system totally unknown until 1967, and possessing for many potholers in its "Passage of Time" one of the best decorated cave passages in the Pennines. Fortunately (for the sake of its preservation), the Passage of Time is way beyond the reach of we mortal travellers, and accessible only to the most experienced, and by all accounts the slimmest, of potholers.*

At Yockenthwaite the main valley line of the Way is regained.

YOCKENTHWAITE to CAM HOUSES
10.2 kilometres (6.4 miles)

Yockenthwaite is a curious name that has puzzled writers down the ages, one found in various guises in the parish registers with one parson writing it simply as "Yoke and White". In 1241 it appeared as "Yoghannesthweit", and here lies a clue to its meaning: "thwaite", of course, is a clearing, while "Yoghannes" proves to be a corruption of the Old Irish personal name, Eogan. So, Yockenthwaite is "Eogan's clearing".

Before pressing on, Yockenthwaite Bridge and the lazy crystal waters of the Wharfe are worth a moment's attention, but do not cross the bridge; return instead towards the main farm building and locate a signposted path going left to a gate, continuing then along the northern bank of the river through level pastures.

Low-flying dippers are a pleasing sight all along the Wharfe, and especially here where open ground provides good viewing of these and the other birds - wagtails, swallows and swifts (in season) - for whom the river is an ideal habitat.

A little further on, between the two communities and close beside the path, a prehistoric stone circle may be found, a compact arrangement of some thirty stones in a delightful riparian setting. The name 'Giant's Grave' was once used locally for the circle, a perfect ring of stones with a few outer stones suggesting that a larger circle, almost certainly long since broken up for walls, once existed. The circle is thought to date from the Bronze Age, and to have been some kind of burial place, but when Bronze Age Man ventured into these wild recesses 3000 years ago, who knows what practices he got up to in stone circles!

After the stone circle the track becomes rather less pronounced, but heads for a stile leading into an enclosed pasture where an indistinct path rises away from the Wharfe, through a gap in a wall and on to a ladder stile to pass round the edge of a field before reaching a small footbridge across Deepdale Gill. Just a short distance further and the access road to Deepdale farm is reached. Follow the track out to the valley road, and cross the Wharfe by Deepdale bridge.

Yockenthwaite. (W.Unsworth)

Approaching Beckermonds.

On the moors near the Cam High Road.
The rolling northern moors of Whernside above Cowgill,
from Arten Gill.

Approaching Beckermonds

Deepdale and Yockenthwaite are virtually identical communities, and must have altered little over the last few centuries, blessed, if not by the privations of their isolation, then by an outstanding and extravagant beauty all around. Once, such an observation would have been a reflection of the prosaic and naive notion of country life held by a visiting urban dweller. Now, many years of wandering on, the eye has learned to look beyond the facade of Nature's novelty to the realities of an often harsh and difficult existence...and still the beauty of the long stretch of river scenery from Buckden to Beckermonds is unsurpassed in all the Dales.

Beyond the bridge a wide path, well defined between wall and water, courts the river as it fusses and gurgles over its smooth bed of limestone. A rickety footbridge near New House has obviously seen better times, and its use (not that it is needed) should not be contemplated. Continue with the river, an idyllic proposition, and one that leads ultimately to the rather larger community of Beckermonds.

Beckermonds, or *Beggarmans*, as some call it, lies in a sheltered hollow, an oasis on the edge of Greenfield Forest. Peacefully it presides over the confluence of Oughtershaw and Greenfield Becks, where the Wharfe can with certainty be said to begin, though its waters derive from much higher and more distant sources we have yet to meet.

This remote hamlet predates the Domesday men for its name derives from the Danes, beckur for stream and mund for mouth.

Just south of Beckermonds a footbridge spans Greenfield Beck, and a short, walled way takes us up to the Beckermonds access road. Turn right along the access road to meet the valley road, and then left up the road as far as Oughtershaw.

Oughtershaw is the last settlement of any size in Wharfedale, and surprisingly sheltered in spite of its elevation (350m: 1150ft), a place where trees grow to full maturity. Indeed its name - Outer Shaw - is very much an appropriate appellation, "shaw" being an Old English word for a wooded area offering shelter and shade.

Between Oughtershaw and Cam the farming must be of the roughest kind, and there is little reason to believe much has changed in hundreds of years so much at one is the community with its surroundings.

In 1499 there were six tenements in Oughtershaw, all connected in some way with the great hunting forest. Of those distant times only a few seventeenth-century buildings remain, while the Tudor-styled Oughtershaw Hall was a latecomer, built about 1850 by Basil George Woodd who lived to be 91 and laboured hard and long to recover much of the surrounding moorland, turning it slowly into meadow and pastureland. Many of his family became ministers of religion, but Basil George was the exception, preferring soil to souls.

Worth a moment's pause too is the school, built in the Venetian style from fine, polished granite, and designed by John Ruskin, while a nearby mock-Celtic cross commemorates Queen Victoria's Jubilee.

Close by the cross the road bends right to begin the trek to Hawes. Here the Way leaves the road for a broad track alongside the river to the austere setting of Nethergill, easily followed and continuing to another remote farmstead, Swarthgill, beyond which the distant cluster of Cam Houses blends greyly into the hillside.

Pass left of the buildings at Swarthgill, and prepare for under-foot conditions that are less than appetising after rain. Just after Swarthgill pass through a gate and then, keeping a wall on the left, pursue a westerly course to Far End Barn (833823).

Three hundred metres before Far End Barn a significant point will have been reached, for here, between the waters of Oughtershaw Beck and Cam Beck the watershed of Britain is crossed. Walkers arriving at this threshold in a contented and enlightened frame of mind will, however, find this geographical titbit hard to believe. Ahead the ground surely rises yet further, beyond Cam Woodlands; how can water possibly flow through that? Yet it does, for there is a distinct optical illusion about the landscape. (Walkers arriving soaked and miserable are excused duty when it comes to marvelling at yet another of Nature's idiosyncrasies.)

A little muddy progress below Breadpiece Barn (830822) leads by a ladder stile to the barn and a short rise to Cam Houses. The path climbs half right before levelling out to reach the first building, where refreshments (and overnight accommodation) may be obtained.

Keep the main building on the right and pass through a gate (right) to gain access to the farm.

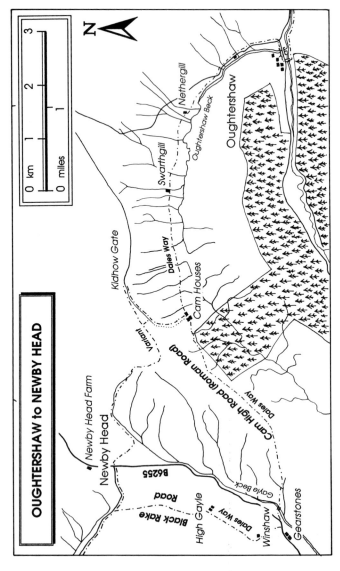

OUGHTERSHAW to NEWBY HEAD

2. Ribblehead and Dentdale

CAM HOUSES

There can be few farms more isolated than Cam, the most remote of the "outside farms" of Wharfedale, tucked away high above the head of Langstrothdale, and in the unique position of gazing out on the wild beginnings both of the Wharfe and the Ribble. Because it lies over the watershed, Cam has an administrative affinity with Ribblesdale, but its spiritual and cultural ties remain firmly bonded to Wharfedale.

At the end of the eighteenth century there were thirteen "livings" at Cam Houses, a neat and mutually supportive community of several farms smaller than those of more recent times. Not surprisingly peat, hewn from the unfathomable moors that emphasise Cam's solitude, was the principal fuel, though some men managed to eke a living from digging coal, while another contrived employment by travelling the outlying farms mending and making shoes.

*In such isolated places the setting is well designed for ghosts, and Cam had two. One a **spectral white dog** known as Jerry and given to haunting the path from the nearby Roman road; the other **"t'owd joiner"**, never seen but often heard hammering away in a room of one of the houses. Here too, it is said, a man once sold his wife for five gold sovereigns, a horse, harness and a cartload of peat; it was by all accounts the filling of the cart with peat that finally clinched the deal!*

CAM HOUSES to HOLME HILL (Gearstones)
4.8 kilometres (3 miles)

The Way now continues through a small wicket gate on the left, ignores the surfaced farm access track departing right, to pass to the left of the last barn to a gate and stile before climbing diagonally up the ensuing hillside to the top corner of a plantation.

A stile in a fence allows access to a very boggy edge of the plantation, where the Way climbs alongside a fence to meet a broad forest trail with a path (signposted) slanting away from it to join an almost parallel fenceline. Follow the fence, left, and cross it at a step stile beyond which a sketchy path continues an upward course to the prominent cairn and marker post on Cam High Road, at 520 metres (1705 feet) the highest point of the Dales Way. Here, along the flanks of Cam Fell, the Dales Way meets the Pennine Way for a very brief encounter lasting a mere 1.8 kilometres (1.1 miles).

*There is some suggestion that **Cam High Road** has prehistoric origins, but it was unquestionably developed and used by the Romans under **General Julius Agricola** as part of his campaigning network of roads, here linking Bainbridge and Ribchester, through the mountainous regions of Britain during his suppression of the Brigantes. Later it was used by wool traders who gave it its name. In the 1750s the route became a turnpike, only to be abandoned for the gentler gradients of Widdale.*

From this high point of the Way and down the Romanesque directness that leads to Holme Hill and Gearstones a splendid view unfolds of Ingleborough, Pen y Ghent and Whernside, Yorkshire's famous "Three Peaks", their purple-blue forms dominating the landscape and serving well to illustrate why between them they were once considered to be the highest mountains in England. In slanting autumnal light, when the bracken has turned to gold and the hills assume a dark steely grey, this wild vantage point bordering the watershed of Britain has a magical, unforgettable quality.

In company with the Pennine Way (southbound), the Dales Way proceeds easily to Cam End, where the two great walks once more pursue their separate destinations. The Dales Way descends uneventfully in a straight line towards Gayle Beck.

Ahead the strong profile of Ingleborough stands stark against the distant skyline, while underfoot may be found numerous fossil-bearing rocks from the time of Britain's submergence beneath a Carboniferous sea, an era that lasted eighty million years and began about 350 million years ago.

A sturdy footbridge, with a rather awkward step up, spans Gayle Beck and leads to a stile by a gate; the remains of an ancient milestone lie beside the gate. A short track leads to the road (B6255) linking Ingleton and Hawes, part of the much longer Lancaster to Richmond road, as another ancient milestone nearby testifies. Follow the road left for a mere 200 metres to a broad track (right, signposted) heading to Winshaw farm.

[The on-going description for the main line of the Dales Way continues on page 73.]

Variant: CAM HOUSES TO NEWBY HEAD VIA THE HIDDEN VALLEY
5.5 kilometres (3.4 miles)

Walkers with no particular reason to head for Holme Hill or Gearstones may find this variant shortcut of interest. It leads into an infrequently visited area of wild moorland, and could save an hour's walking.

Leave Cam Houses by its surfaced access road and climb to Cam High Road. The two roads meet beneath a prominent cairn on the edge of a limestone scar. Turn right along Cam High Road and go as far as Kidhow Gate, here turning acutely left to enter a broad, walled cul-de-sac with a gate on the right. Many of the rocks forming the walls here contain oceanic fossils in great number.

Beyond the gate bear obliquely left across trackless, peaty ground to a collapsed wall, and then climb on to the broad expanse of a grass-covered limestone plateau. A broad green path, later reducing to little more than a sheep track, heads west-northwest across the plateau aiming for Gavel Gap (813832). In poor visibility a bearing west will intersect the wall then leading northwest to Gavel Gap, which has been substantially sealed by building blocks, but with enough room for walkers to continue on to the path beyond. (Walkers should note that between Kidhow Gate and Gavel Gap there is no apparent right of way, and should be prepared to abandon plans to use this variant if circumstances make it advisable. Even so, the paths that do exist are in regular use by walkers and are detailed in a number of publications, not that such a qualification necessarily confirms their status.)

From Gavel Gap follow a path (this time a legitimate right of way) along the line of Jam Sike, swinging round and down into the Hidden Valley, a wild and unsuspected moorland retreat splendidly framing the bulk of distant Ingleborough. Cross the stream where Jam Sike meets Long Gill and continue along a narrow path to an isolated shed (shelter in emergency,

71

but only if you are desperate!).

Continue around the shed to relocate the path which now swings northwest to reach the B6255, at Newby Head, near its junction with the Dent/Sedbergh road. Follow this road until the Dales Way joins it from the left at 786836 (see, however, the variant from Newby Head to Dentdale via Wold Fell and Great Knoutberry Hill detailed below).

GEARSTONES

A short way along the Hawes-Ingleton road, once a Roman road and later a stretch of the Richmond turnpike constructed during the 1750s, stands Gearstones, offering walkers a night's bed and breakfast as well as bunkhouse accommodation.

During the eighteenth century, in the days of the Scottish drovers, Gearstones was a thriving wayside inn. Here, at the end of a long drovers' haul south via Mallerstang and Widdale, Scottish longhorns would be gathered for sale, twice a year. Over the bustling scene would drift the smell of burning peat, as hundreds of cattle crowded into pens, yappy dogs, tired lads, English buyers and Scottish sellers all jostled for space. As the evening wore on business haggling would gradually come to an end and a weary state of drunkenness settled on everyone, many drovers sleeping rough in their plaids sheltering against the walls. A couple of miles away across the moors, Newby Head, then also an inn, was where the butchers were to be found. Great sheep fairs were also held on Malham Moor or at Skipton market, a tradition that was to continue throughout the eighteenth century into the nineteenth, and a way of life that ended only with the coming of the railways.

※ ※ ※

The Dales Way continues from the old turnpike road across the eastern slopes of Blea Moor to descend into Dentdale, a fairly simple and ultimately speedy stretch involving a measure of roadwalking. On this occasion the idea of a roadwalk is quite a pleasant proposition, for Dentdale, and upper Dentdale in particular, has a rare beauty, green, fertile, a welcome place of seclusion, surrounded by steep-sided fells.

Walkers wanting to stay at **Denthead Youth Hostel** (Deeside House, formerly a shooting lodge) of necessity must go this way.

Two variants, however, suggest themselves; one crossing from Newby Head to Wold Fell and Great Knoutberry Hill; the other following the Craven Way, an ancient packhorse route between Settle and Hawes, and making rather more directly for Dent. These variants are detailed on pages 77-78 and 78-81 respectively.

HOLME HILL (Gearstones) to MILL BRIDGE
12.6 kilometres (7.9 miles)

Leave the B6255 at the broad track (signposted) leading to Winshaw Farm. Some footpath re-routing takes the Way up to the left of the farm on to the moor, bearing right at the top corner of a wall to start a near level traverse of Gayle Moor. The route stays with the wall until, just after High Gayle Farm, it drops away; here, keep straight on to meet and turn left along an improving track. Quite likely constructed by the builders of the railway, this is a pleasant track, which ambles along easily round the edge of Gayle Moor, occasionally losing its way in bent grasses and bog, but never desperately so. Some maps give this track the name Black Rake Road; it finally meets the Newby road at 786836. En route, as the first of two fences in quick succession is encountered, the Dales Way says goodbye to Yorkshire and enters Cumbria; whether it has the feel of Cumbria is quite another matter. From the county boundary the path does its best to avoid the wettest stretches of Stoops Moss before reaching the road at a stile.

Walkers who have used the variant route from Cam Houses into the Hidden Valley will join the Newby road at its junction with the B6255, and should then use Newby road to link the two points. Now all that remains is to follow the road to Lea Yeat bridge, near Cowgill.

Walkers bound for the youth hostel are effectively compelled to travel this way, though a more circuitous route following the line of the engineers' path above Blea Moor tunnel could be devised without too much difficulty. Other accommodation can also be found in this upper section of Dentdale, and good progress can be made if time is pressing a little.

Continue down the road, first encountering a steep descent to pass beneath the arches of Dent Head viaduct, behind which

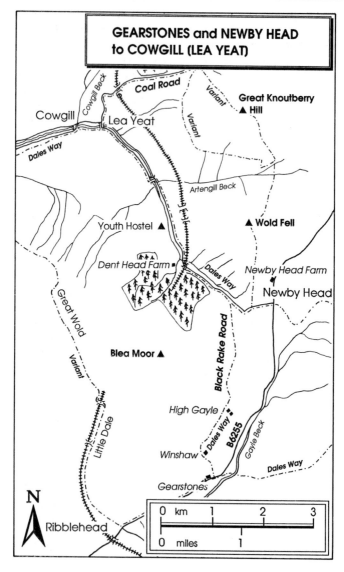

GEARSTONES and NEWBY HEAD
to COWGILL (LEA YEAT)

Coal Road

Great Knoutberry
▲ Hill

Cowgill

Cowgill Beck

Lea Yeat

Variant

Variant

Dales Way

Artengill Beck

▲ Wold Fell

Youth Hostel ▲

Dent Head Farm ■

Dales Way

Newby Head Farm

Newby Head

Great Wold

Black Rake Road

Blea Moor ▲

Variant

Little Dale

High Gayle

Dales Way

B6255

Gayle Beck

Winshaw

Dales Way

Gearstones

N

Ribblehead

| 0 | km | 1 | | 2 | | 3 |

| 0 | miles | | 1 | |

there is a now disused bridge spanning Fell End Gill, one of the feeder streams that make up the start of the River Dee which will now accompany our journey until it meets the River Lune.

Passing the youth hostel the river flows over long flat stretches of limestone bedrock from which it has fashioned its own cascading course, spilling over short underwater ledges to prove a constant and lively companion in all but the driest conditions, when it is likely to disappear underground for a good deal of its length. Scow Force waterfall is just a rather larger limestone ledge than others (nearby **Scow Cottage**, B&B, was formerly a railway workers' cottage), while **Stone House**, just before the junction with Arten Gill, used to be a sizeable nineteenth-century marble works, capitalising on the local abundance of the much-prized black **"Dent marble"**. Though no longer popular, Dent marble was once extensively used for interior decorative purposes, especially as polished mantelpieces and ornamental columns. It isn't marble at all, of course, but a limestone with a high carbon content, and one that will make a fine paperweight should you find a suitable piece.

At Stone House the road crosses the river and continues downwards, to the small hamlet of Cowgill, where it changes banks once more.

As soon as we reach Lea Yeat bridge we leave the road by a stile to gain a footpath on the south bank of the river, following this soon to reach Ewegales Bridge. Now turn left up a narrow road, pass Ewegales Farm and then go left through a gate into a broad sloping pasture. Make for the farm buildings of Rivling, but keep below them and press on ahead to a stile giving access to a spruce plantation.

The path through the plantation is not among the best along the Way, floundering about as it does from one boggy patch to another, but only for a short time. Quite unexpectedly the path approaches Little Town, where it is diverted via stiles to pass to the right of the buildings, to maintain an element of privacy. Cross the access track to another stile for a second dose of plantation. Towards the end the path rises to meet two stiles by means of which it escapes from the trees, and then follows the line of a wall to meet another access track beyond a stile.

Follow this access track, slightly uphill, for a short distance, and then branch right across a minor stream to another stile before pressing on to meet the access track to Hackergill and Coat Faw, near which we get our first view of Dent and distant Combe Scar.

Looking ahead throughout this stretch there are good views down the valley with Great Coum and Middleton Fell particularly prominent. It is easy, too, to recognise the influence the Viking invaders who cleared and settled the valley, setting up scattered homesteads along the spring line, to ensure a ready supply of fresh water, and to keep their dwellings away from the often water-logged valley bottoms. The walking on this section of the Way, and for that matter on both sides of the valley, is very much affected by these scattered dwellings, twisting and turning all the while, yet never proving arduous.

Near Coat Faw a ladder stile gives access to a small meadow at the far side of which another, taller, ladder stile puts us on a path passing beneath a prominent scar (wall on the right). Approaching Clint the path is deflected around the back of the buildings, and then drops to a stile and a gate in a half-concealed corner to resume a level walk, now with a wall on the left. Pass West Clint, using its access track, and at the corner of the field leave the track for a stile, continuing past a barn and crossing a small stream.

Just beyond the stream aim right to pass round a large barn, immediately joining the access to Laithbank and turning right to descend to a road. Go left along this minor road, which is the one last encountered at Ewegales, until just past a house, Tub Hole, on the left. Here turn right through a gate into a field. Continue across the field to the prominent tree-lined ravine of Lenny's Leap, passing to the right of it to rejoin the river at Nelly Bridge, a narrow and hidden footbridge spanning the river.

Cross the bridge and go left, heading downriver, and pass by several stiles finally to reach another footbridge, Tommy Bridge, back over the Dee. Walkers bound for Whernside Centre should go left here and up to join the minor road again, from where the Centre lies to the right (see below). The Dales Way however goes immediately right once across Tommy Bridge, through a gate. At a second gate cross a stile on the left and leave the river once more, to climb beside a right hand wall. Keep on ahead, aiming to the left of an attractive group of trees, climbing a low hillside, and then aiming (initially unsighted) for a stile near Bridge End Farm at Mill bridge (720861).

[The on-going description of the main line of the Dales Way between Mill Bridge and Dent continues on page 81].

Variants
Walkers wishing to avoid the long roadwalk between Newby Head and Cowgill may do so by either of two possible alternative routes, both longer and rather more demanding, but with splendid open views and the full repertoire of dirty tricks normally associated with moorland wandering.

Variant 1: NEWBY HEAD GATE TO LEA YEAT (Cowgill) VIA WOLD FELL AND GREAT KNOUTBERRY HILL
Via Great Knoutberry Hill: 7 kilometres (4.4 miles)
Via Galloway Gate: 8 kilometres (5 miles)

From Newby Head Gate (791835) on the Newby road a bridleway (signposted: "Wold Fell") follows the county boundary to the fell's flat limestone top, and offers fine views into the surrounding dales and of the Three Peaks. The signpost, however, also tells you that the route is a "dead end", culminating as it does not far from the summit. A path of sorts does continue to the top of Arten Gill, but though in use for many years, is not a right of way; it meets the track from Stone House to Widdale after a gentle skirmish with Arten Gill Moss.

From this point there are two possibilities: one is to continue ahead following a wall and climbing in a seemingly endless series of boggy steps to the top of Great Knoutberry Hill, from where a nearby fence may be crossed easily and the line of a long since collapsed fence followed northwestwards to meet the Coal Road at 779881. None of this is along rights of way; but again, as evidenced by the established pathways, the line has been in use for many years.

The second possibility descends left a little from the top of Arten Gill, until, not far from a gate, it meets a broad and stony track climbing right. This is an old drove road known as

Galloway Gate, mainly used by farmers droving from the Galloway Hills, hence its name. This, of course, is a legal right of way, and sweeps round the flank of Great Knoutberry Hill to meet the Coal Road at a gate.

The road carries the name "Coal Road" because it once served small bell pits and shallow workings near the top of the pass, an important source of fuel for Dent Town.

From the gate turn left and descend the minor road, finishing steeply just above Cowgill village, near Lea Yeat bridge.

Variant 2: HOLME HILL (Gearstones) TO MILL BRIDGE VIA THE CRAVEN WAY
11.8 kilometres (7.4 miles)

The Craven Way, an ancient packhorse route linking Ribblesdale and Dentdale, offers one of the loveliest stretches of green track in Northern England, with panoramic views along the length of Dentdale to the Howgills.

Go left along the B6255 towards Ribblehead. A shortcut across the southern limestone fringe of Blea Moor is unlikely in clear conditions to cause anyone to go astray, but by continuing to Ribblehead it becomes possible to inspect at close hand one of the greatest achievements of the Victorian era, the Ribblehead Viaduct. This involves a little over 2 kilometres (1¼ miles) of roadwalking with the bulk of Ingleborough looming ahead, Pen y Ghent away to the left, trying to get in on the act, and, gradually, the highest of the Three Peaks, Whernside, taking its place, off to the right.

On reaching Ribblehead start along the broad track that leaves the B6255 at 764791, and follow this to the foot of the viaduct.

The railway that crosses the viaduct, the Settle-Carlisle line, is a stark reminder of the Midland Railway's determination to construct its own route to Scotland. The viaduct, constructed in the early 1870s, was built at enormous cost both in terms of finance and of human life; over 100 navvies who worked on its construction and the associated Blea Moor tunnel, lie buried in the churchyard of St Leonard's, Chapel-le-Dale.

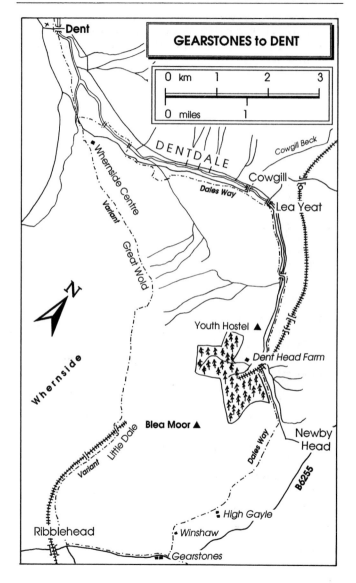

GEARSTONES to DENT

0 km 1 2 3

0 miles 1

Dent

DENTDALE

Cowgill Beck

Whernside Centre

Variant

Great Wold

Dales Way

Cowgill

Lea Yeat

N

Whernside

Youth Hostel ▲

Dent Head Farm

Blea Moor ▲

Little Dale

Variant

Dales Way

Newby Head

B6255

High Gayle

Winshaw

Gearstones

Ribblehead

In recent years, affected by the ravages of time and the sheer aggressiveness of the climate in these parts, the future of the railway was called into question as the spectre of financial viability reared its head. During this period a vigorous campaign was waged to keep the line open, and all the effort that went into the campaign was at last vindicated when, in April, 1989, the Government announced that the line was to remain open. During the early 1990s the viaduct saw massive and much-needed repair work, funded by a consortium comprising British Rail, English Heritage, local authorities and other interested bodies.

A broad track continues beneath the arches of the viaduct, but the Dales Way ignores this. Continue instead on a signposted path along the east side of the railway, pass Blea Moor sidings and signal box, to Little Dale Beck. The beck can be awkward to cross after prolonged rain, but once beyond it we soon come to a fine curiosity of the route, a double bridge over the railway. One part of the bridge carries the path, while another part channels the waters of Force Gill into Little Dale Beck.

Now a steady climb begins, with experiments in footpath repair work, in this case intermittent boarding, making progress rather easier than it would otherwise be. When a signpost is reached (here the track goes left to reach the northern end of Whernside's summit ridge) continue ahead for Dentdale, soon to swing around the northern flank of Whernside to gaze down on the length of Dentdale. Once Wold End is reached all is downhill, the Craven Way rocketing towards Dent in an almost straight line, finally reaching the valley near Whernside Centre.

Whernside Centre, now more correctly Whernside Outdoor Recreation and Study Centre, shown on maps as Whernside Manor, was originally West House, and reputedly built by slave labour by the Sill family who were Jamaican slave traders during the late eighteenth-century. The present-day study centre has evolved from a former Caving Centre, and offers a wide range of imaginative and adventurous courses which look at various aspects of Dales life.

Right: Dent Town (W. Unsworth)

The Howgills seen from the banks of the Rawthey.
Looking back at Field Close and the fells around Staveley

(Details may be obtained from the Manager, Whernside Centre, Dent, Sedbergh, Cumbria, LA10 5RE. Send a stamped addressed envelope.)

On reaching a minor road turn left, and shortly right on Dyke Hall Lane, to meet the main valley road which should be followed, left, to Mill Bridge.

MILL BRIDGE to DENT (Church Bridge)
2 kilometres (1.25 miles)

Cross the bridge and go into the trees on the right, following a path that courts Deepdale Beck as far as its confluence with the Dee. Now follow the path along the banks of the Dee until, just before Church Bridge, flood embankments divert the path left to cross a minor stream, beyond which the path goes right, continuing by stiles to Church Bridge.

Dent village lies up the road to the left.

DENT

Dent, properly Dent Town, is a place of beauty, and even walkers not intending to overnight there must not miss it for the sake of an hour or so. It has most things a wayfarer might need: accommodation, shops, cafés, inns and toilets. A place where cobbled streets reek of interest and closely-packed houses fight for space; a place that shimmers with individuality.

A twelfth-century church, dedicated to St Andrew, is worth a visit in itself. It probably came under the care of the monks at Coverham Abbey, near Middleham. Rebuilding became necessary in 1417, and yet more restoration followed in 1590, 1787 and 1889. Whether the restoration was needed from natural causes, or as a result of drunken brawling one begins to wonder when you glance at the Church records. In 1760 items on the church account were:

> *"3 quarts of wine on Whit Sunday*
> *7 quarts of wine at Michaelmas*
> *6 quarts of wine at Christmas (and an incredible)*
> *4 gallons of wine at Easter"*

Once described as a "Terrestrial paradise" (and no wonder!), there is still ample reason to think of Dent in the same terms. There is, too, a curious tendency to longevity among Dent citizens. In 1664 a father and son were subpoenaed to the Assizes at York; one is recorded as being 140 and the other 100. The burial register of 1817 shows that one Elizabeth King lived to be 111; now, the French have this conviction that drinking wine prolongs active life, so to speak...makes you wonder if the people of Dentdale had cottoned on to that, as well.

On one corner a huge fountain carved from a block of granite commemorates **Adam Sedgwick (1785-1873)**, *son of the town, born at the Old Parsonage, a great Victorian geologist whose work laid the foundations for modern geological studies. For more than fifty years he was Woodwardian Professor of Geology at Cambridge, though, according to one account, when the professorship became vacant Sedgwick was practically ignorant of the subject, whilst his rival for the post, a G.C. Gorham, was known to have studied it extensively. By whatever means, Sedgwick was elected by 186 votes to 59, and only on his election as professor did he begin to study the subject. Later he was elected President of the Geological Society, President of the British Association and in 1834 became a Canon of Norwich Cathedral.*

Many of the taller houses in the main street of Dent once had first-floor galleries where local knitters, who formed a thriving cottage industry, would sit knitting simple garments from which Dentdale ultimately derived its share of fame. Now, alas, only the cobbled streets, the church, and a few plaques and monuments tell of those distant times.

✳ ✳ ✳

CHURCH BRIDGE (Dent) to MILLTHROP (Sedbergh)
8 kilometres (5 miles)

Descend the steps at Church Bridge to regain the Way along the top of flood banks; finally emerge on and follow the Sedbergh road for a short distance to a bench (700874), where a step stile leads back to the riverside. An obvious green path (wet in places, especially near field boundaries) leads to Barth Bridge and a flight of steps ascending to the road (see the variant below for an alternative link between Barth Bridge and Sedbergh Golf Course).

To the south of Dent village rises the mound of Great Coum and Crag Hill, and shortly after leaving Church Bridge there is an especially pleasing view of the village against this mountain backdrop. Prominent are the

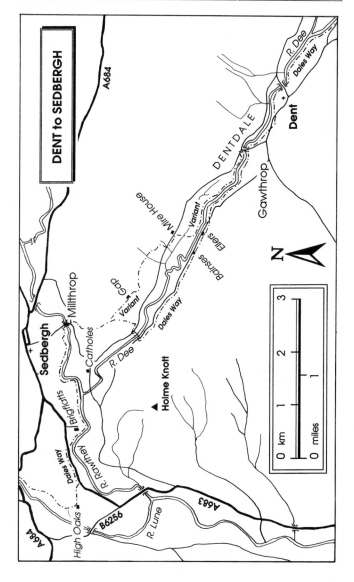

DENT to SEDBERGH

83

Megger Stones (704851), a group of cairns on the slopes of Great Coum.

Cross the road as it reaches Barth Bridge and descend more steps once again to edge round a field with hedgerows, trees and low scrub between the path and the river, well patrolled by dippers and grey wagtails.

The next objective is the farm, Ellers. Between Barth Bridge and Ellers the Way follows the river closely, often using flood banks, and passing through a slippery wooded section where for a while walking commands greater attention than the charms of the surrounding countryside. Stretches of the path are overgrown in summer, narrow and often muddy, and on a wet day gaiters or waterproof overtrousers will prove helpful.

That the countryside around has great charm is beyond doubt, the water meadows between Barth Bridge and Rash once formed a glacial lake, and from time to time still flood. To the northeast rises the low ridge of Aye Gill Pike, separating Dentdale from Garsdale and the sprawling expanse of Baugh Fell, while southwest the secluded vale of Barbondale slices through the landscape below Calf Top.

At Ellers (679886), the Way joins a pleasant and quiet back road for the stretch to Rash Bridge where the route swings right and finally crosses the Dee.

When next the Dee is encountered, near Birks Mill, it will have joined forces with the Rawthey, that, too, shortly to be consumed by the Lune.

Cross Rash Bridge and climb gently to a road junction. Turn right along the main valley road for a short distance to a gate, on the left, just before Rash Farm (signposted: "Millthrop"). Head up the centre of a field to a stile, then, following the wall upwards, seek out a concealed stile at the edge of a small copse (662904).

This final section to the copse marks the last opportunity to take in the extensive view down Dentdale. We seem to have whizzed through it, and must now start turning our thoughts to the Lune and the fringes of the Lake District. Strong walkers could manage the crossing from Cam Houses to Sedbergh comfortably in one day, but that would be a little too hasty, and not really according Dentdale the consideration it deserves. Back across the valley the dark crags of Combe Scar contrast sharply with the rich greenness of the pastureland below, and the pity is that Dentdale is woefully short. But we haven't quite finished with it yet.

From the copse a short, narrow path leads to a wider track between walls. At a gate continue ahead, and as the path forks, keep right alongside the wall to a stile on the edge of **Sedbergh Golf Course**. Follow a broad track across the golf course to the club house.

*A moment's pause near the golf club house will not go amiss, for now the great swell of the **Howgills** rise ahead beyond the Rawthey valley, dominating the town of Sedbergh, and in autumnal light shimmering like shot silk. Here the landscape changes noticeably, and it becomes apparent that the countryside ahead is much different from the Dales country behind. This dramatic transformation is caused by the Dent Fault, a geological slip that cut off the limestones and gritstones of the Carboniferous Series and exposed older Silurian slates. Founded on different bedrock the scenery becomes closer in form to that of the Lake District; the vegetation contains subtle changes, the field walls are constructed of markedly different materials, as, too, are the buildings.*

Follow the golf course access road down its stony length to **Millthrop**. Turn right to enter this charming village, past its curiously-shaped **Primitive Methodist Church**, and in a few strides go left to a T-junction, and right to **Millthrop Bridge** for a first glimpse of the Rawthey.

(Walkers breaking their journey at Sedbergh, should continue ahead beyond Millthrop Bridge, noting on the left just after the bridge the kissing gate, signposted: "Birks", that marks the resumption of the Way.)

[The on-going description for the main line of the Dales Way continues on page 89.]

Variant: BARTH BRIDGE TO SEDBERGH GOLF COURSE
Church Bridge to Millthrop: 7.25 kilometres (4.5 miles)

Cross Barth Bridge and follow the road for about 400 metres to a path, left (signposted: "Mire House"). Leave the road and descend to the right bank of the Dee, with open meadows and a fine view of Helms Knott on the right. Press on to Ellers footbridge; remain on the right bank and at the second stile turn right to cross a field to a stile and then obliquely left across pastureland to rejoin the road opposite Mire House. Turn left and follow the road as far as Craggs Farm. Opposite the farm leave the road and keep ahead up the field (don't go left through a tempting gap) to a concealed squeeze stile in a wall on the left.

Ahead lies Leakses Farm. Cross the field (no obvious path), keeping well below an outfall of farm slurry, to a step stile. Go left to meet the main farm access road and then sharp right to a gate on the left. Traverse the ensuing field to a gap in a wall and then on to a ladder stile just before Burton Hill Farm. Pass through the farm yard to a wrought iron gate, and then left as you enter the next field, keeping to the lower end of the field to a squeeze stile next to a gate. As you cross the next field Hewthwaite Farm comes into view.

The way across the field is indistinct, but by aiming for the gable of the left-hand building a squeeze stile will be found, giving on to the farm access. Keep ahead through a gate and by stone stiles (not always obvious) to an isolated farm building, Gap (667900). Beyond the building, continue to a gate and on to Gap Wood. The way through Gap Wood is obvious and leads on to a broad track that the main route joins at the copse (662904), just before the golf course.

SEDBERGH and the HOWGILLS

The cloak of anonymity that has settled on Sedbergh gives it a pleasant if plain air, though it saves the town the over frequent attention of tourists. It is an ancient market town (its charter dates from 1251) with a mention in the Domesday Book as among the numerous manors held by Earl Tostig of Northumbria, one of the sons of Earl Godwin of Wessex and brother of King Harold. Today its fame rests on the laurels of its school which began in 1525 and has grown steadily to become a place with a national reputation.

Here we are on the very edge of the Dales, pressing hard against the rolling fells of Lakeland; indeed was it not the Lakeland affinity that was in the planners' minds when in 1974 they ceded Sedbergh to Cumbria from its hitherto placid existence tucked away in the northwestern extremity of the West Riding of Yorkshire?

Yet in spite of its administrative links with Cumbria, Sedbergh remains as the largest town in the Yorkshire Dales National Park, the main western gateway to the Dales. Towards the end of the eighteenth century the Turnpike Acts of 1761 brought improvements to the Askrigg-Kendal and Lancaster-Kirkby Stephen roads, both of which pass through Sedbergh. These improvements, making the town more easily accessible, and a period of industrial growth as the local domestic knitting trade was augmented by a cotton industry based on mills at Birks, Howgill and Millthrop, meant that Sedbergh grew at the expense of Dent, until then the more important township, and one that also relied on its knitting trade to support its economic well-being.

Dominating the town as much as its school's reputation are the Howgills, a fine, rounded selection of hills to satisfy any walker's needs. They lie to the north of the town, encompassed by the rivers Rawthey and Lune, the latter rising on the northern extremity of the range and sweeping round, north, west and south to pass Sedbergh by. Few walls or fences tame these fells, where wild horses roam free and the call of buzzard, curlew and golden plover are ever on the air.

(Walkers with time to spend a few days in Sedbergh will find the author's book *The Pennine Mountains* details eleven fine excursions into the Howgills, a number of them starting from or near Sedbergh.)

✳ ✳ ✳

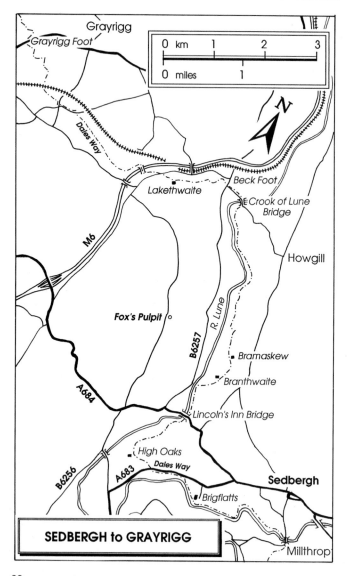

SEDBERGH to GRAYRIGG

3. Lonsdale and the Lakeland Fringe

MILLTHROP (Sedbergh) to LINCOLN'S INN BRIDGE
5.8 kilometres (3.6 miles)

Just north of Millthrop Bridge a path (signposted: "Birks") starts
(west) through a kissing gate. Set off along this, swinging right
across the ensuing field to a squeeze stile behind a wooden gate
giving access to a small copse. The path trends right in the wood
at a walled trench, making for another kissing gate by which the
copse is left. (Note: There are other paths through the wood, going
left, that lead closer to the River Rawthey and continue in the right
direction, but these are not part of the Way.)

On leaving the copse, turn left with the fence and climb a knoll
to pass to the right of a ruined edifice that seems to be a relic of the
Second World War. From this raised vantage point there is a fine
view northwards to the Howgills. Now go ahead down a field
to a stile almost back on the riverbank, and follow the edge of
Sedbergh School rugby grounds to a stile in a dip. Climb easily
past a solitary house, soon to reach a minor road between Birks
and Sedbergh.

Go left along the road, through the tiny hamlet of Birks and as
far as Birks Mill, a former cotton mill, where a footbridge spans
the Rawthey, giving access to Catholes and its bunkhouse barn.
Keep left of the mill and continue to a stile returning the path to
the riverbank. Press on through another small copse from which
the final appearance of the River Dee may be seen, having
accompanied the Way since its birth high on the bleak slopes of
Blea Moor, Wold Fell and Great Knoutberry Hill, now losing
itself as it joins forces with the Rawthey.

Pleasant pastures ensue as the Way approaches the embankment of the former Ingleton-Tebay branch railway. Cross the
embankment and descend on a narrow path through nettles,
brambles and wild raspberries along the edge of a field to a
stile. The path courts the Rawthey for a while longer as far as

Brigflatts, beyond which it follows a path tight between barbed wire fence and river. As the Rawthey, too, takes its leave, swinging southwest for its imminent encounter with the Lune, follow the path to reach the A683.

Brigflatts, once a small flax-weavers' settlement, is a seemingly innocuous group of farm buildings, but among them is a quite historic building, the Friends Meeting House, a small and beautiful white cottage, gazing out over the Rawthey with unassuming grace, and built as a cooperative effort in 1675, at a time when nonconformist meetings were illegal and failure to attend parish church brought persecution. It is claimed that one dalesman never attended a Friends' meeting without taking his nightcap, in case he was apprehended and sent off to gaol. For consorting with his fellow Christians here on a Sabbath, Alexander Hebblethwaite was fined eight shillings, which he refused to pay and so forfeited his cow. For the same misdemeanour, Richard Robinson, a local blacksmith, was relieved of his tools of trade.

Not surprisingly a faith like Quakerism flourished in these quiet backwaters, where man's solitude, the close presence of mountains and moorland, and the forces of nature, so constantly in evidence, combined to induce a seriousness and introspection in the most extrovert of individuals. When, in June 1652, George Fox, whose preaching, praying and protesting were instrumental in gathering the Society of Friends, came to preach on nearby Firbank Fell fresh from his vision on Pendle Hill, the peaceable people of Sedbergh were more than ready to embrace his religious ideology, finding his words much to their liking. Some three hundred years on this the second oldest meeting house in England is still in use, and, being found by bearing right from the Way by a steep path past the farm buildings, well worth a short diversion.

Go left along the A683 for 600 metres to a double stile through the hedgerow on the right (signposted: "High Oaks"), and follow a fence ahead to a concrete bridge spanning the tiny Haverah Beck. Pass round a small knoll (a knollock, perhaps?) and cross the meadow, aiming for a gap in a hedge. On reaching the gap (signpost: "FP") follow the hedge to a gate giving on to a delightful green lane flanked by hedgerows of bramble, hawthorn and holly. At the end of the lane go right, through a gate, and at the next gate, left into the charming retreat of High Oaks. Almost immediately go right for about 30 metres, then right again (signpost: "FP") along a farm cart track.

Follow the track until confronted by a gate, stile on the left, and three-way signpost. The Way is now heading for Luneside Farm, and follows the right edge of the field. Ignore a step stile on the right and continue across the field to a farm gate. A broad path continues, flanked on the left by a tall hedgerow, and on the right by the remains of walls and hedgerows until at a gate it enters a lane leading directly to Luneside Farm. This lane is frequently used by cows, is invariably very muddy, and extremely well fertilised! With some relief Luneside Farm is reached to the sound of barking dogs.

Stay on the farm access track for a short distance to a gate on the left (signpost: "FP: Across field to tree and then follow fence"). Comply with these instructions, and along the fence watch for a low step stile on the left. A better path ensues as the Way reaches a signpost for Lincoln's Inn Bridge that could more usefully be positioned near the stile, which is easily missed.

Now make for the Lune and accompany it to Lincoln's Inn Bridge, leaving the pasture by a stile adjoining the bridge, and on to the A684.

Lincoln's Inn Bridge is a fine double-arched construction, with the Lune for a while relatively calm and smooth, but above and below the bridge seeming to flex its muscles in anticipation of more energetic passages downstream. The inn, now a farm, with a small adjoining camp site, once served travellers and drovers waiting to ford the river in the days before the bridge was built. "Lincoln" was a former landlord, and no doubt a popular man.

LINCOLN'S INN BRIDGE to CROOK OF LUNE BRIDGE
5.3 kilometres (3.3 miles)

The section of the Dales Way between Lincoln's Inn Bridge and Crook of Lune Bridge is unfairly short, barely enough to hint at the delights of Lonsdale country before we are having to leave it and head for Lakeland. To its credit, this modest contribution to the Dales Way, which forms the northwest boundary of the Yorkshire Dales National Park, does its best to spoil and charm us with exquisite views of the Howgills in particular, set to the rippling accompaniment of the River Lune itself. And in that respect it achieves a notable success, pampering our senses, especially in autumn when the bold bronze domes of the Howgills forever draw our eye, and in spring, when curlews and golden plovers call, and every hedgerow and field is alive with bright-eyed flowers.

We resume our journey by turning right at Lincoln's Inn Bridge onto the A684, towards Sedbergh, leaving the road almost immediately at a gate on the left (signposted: "Low Branthwaite"). Cross the ensuing pasture, following its left edge, and close by the river, which here argues with a rocky constriction. The Lune viaduct soon appears ahead, and off to the right a narrow underpass is seen, about which more in a moment.

By any standards the viaduct is a magnificent piece of architecture, beautifully constructed, but now gazing dolefully redundant out across its valley. Before it is reached, however, we cross a ladder stile and come to a small stream that when in spate will bring a moment's pause. At another ladder stile a choice of routes occurs, both of which have seen some rerouting in recent years. Beyond the ladder stile lies Crosdale Beck, a modest watercourse but one that can be difficult to cross, especially laden with packs. If you do elect to go this way, pass beneath the arches of the viaduct to follow a track across a field before swinging right and up to join a path heading towards Low Branthwaite Farm.

A rather easier proposition, particularly if Crosdale Beck is flowing fast, involves turning right along a wall before crossing the ladder stile, and continuing uphill, following the outside perimeter of a small copse until you can reach the railway underpass. In fact, there used to be a footpath on the other side of the wall, but this was diverted in 1991 to leave the copse free for development as a nature reserve.

Go through the underpass to a gate, and left after the gate, with the first Luneside glimpse of the Howgills suddenly appearing. Follow the field left to a gate, and there turn right to traverse the top edge of a steeply sloping field. Gradually the pasture narrows and eventually we come to a meeting of paths, a mini crossroads.

At the crossroads descend left to a step stile in a corner, and so reach the farm access to Low Branthwaite. Move ahead for a short distance to a signpost pointing out a ladder stile on the right. Cross the stile, heading for Bramaskew, and continue on a pleasant path until you can go left to an iron gate. Just before the gate a signpost and a yellow marker have you turning right, stepping over a low barbed wire fence, that has a modicum of protection taped to it, and following a hawthorn hedge away until it becomes enclosed by a wall on the right. The wall is short-lived, but the path swings round to the left, keeping to a shallow gully. Becoming enclosed once more the path reaches a gate. Pass through the gate and continue on a path between walls, with excellent, inspiring views of the Howgills away to the right.

At a gate a prominent sign ("Dales Way") fixed to a tree catches the eye, and close by you will find a narrow gap stile. Keep the farm, Bramaskew, on your right and follow a fence-cum-hedgerow, looking for another stile. Near an electricity supply line continue ahead, following the line of the overhead cables to a barn concealed in a dip. Keep left at the barn to pass between walls no longer serving any purpose, and then continue away from the barn to meet another wall, soon leading to a double gate. Cross a stream and enter another enclosed way at a gate leading directly to Nether Bainbridge Farm.

Just as we approach Nether Bainbridge we encounter a storage shed and then a barn. A signpost on the left points out the onward route across a stone squeeze stile. Go right, round the barn to another wall with a signpost ("Hole House"), and a small gate.

Do not go through the small gate, but continue left past a gate in a slight projection of the wall and move ahead keeping the wall on the right to another gate with a footpath sign. Climb the modest brow now facing for a really magnificent view of the Howgills from Fell Head, round by The Calf to Arant Haw and Winders. From the top of the hill head directly for Hole House Farm, nestling in a hollow by the river. At the farm gate go ahead into the farmyard, turning right as barns are reached. A short way further on the Way dips to the left, passing between the residential part of the farm on a cobbled way leading to a gate; only a few yellow markers confirm we are on the right line which for a moment has an uneasy, invasionary feel about it.

At the gate descend into a wooded gully to a footbridge across Smithy Beck. Follow the signposted path to Crook of Lune

Bridge, this is the lower of two paths leading to a step stile. In the next meadow a green path swings away to the right, beneath Thwaite Farm, but the Way actually makes for the river, renewing our acquaintance after a short spell away from it. Go ahead at a collapsed wall between two hawthorns and follow the Lune. Another footbridge is crossed, with the Way now remaining clear and staying with the river for some distance, in and out of woodland, up and down a little, until, after a longish straight stretch with a steep embankment on the right, we reach a track leading right to a gate below Crook of Lune Farm.

Beyond the gate follow the track away to meet a wall and then ahead again keeping the wall and a hawthorn hedge on the right. Now a green path takes us on, the Lune viaduct away to the left and Crook of Lune Bridge for the moment out of sight in a hollow. At a gate (stile) a minor road is reached, leading downwards and left to Crook of Lune Bridge.

CROOK OF LUNE BRIDGE to BURNESIDE
13.2 kilometres (8.4 miles)

The River Lune has been the Way's companion since leaving Sedbergh, and it is regrettable that the route does not remain in its company for a little longer. Rising as a few insignificant springs northeast of the summit of Green Bell in the Howgills, the Lune soon sweeps westward, gathering momentum with graceful restraint until, at Tebay, it finds a southerly course and sets off with renewed vigour, bound for Lancaster and the southern edge of Morecambe Bay. In the vicinity of the Crook of Lune Bridge, the river used to form the boundary between the former West Riding of Yorkshire and the sadly defunct county of Westmorland. Thankfully, no amount of bureaucratic carving can affect the resident beauty of the Lune, at a complete contrast with the steady roar of road traffic on the nearby M6 motorway, and the high speed trains that hurtle past on the main London-Glasgow line.

If George Stephenson had been allowed his way, there may never have been a main line railway through the Lune gorge, for in 1837 he (and for that matter John Hague a year later) proposed that the main west coast line should resort to embankments sweeping across Morecambe Bay and along the West Cumberland plain. Officialdom however decreed a more direct, if steeper, route through the Lune gorge, and in 1844 Joseph Locke began the truly incredible feat of taking what was then to be the **Lancaster and Carlisle Railway** *over Shap Fell. Consuming little more than two years in construction, the line was open for traffic in December 1846, and involved a workforce of some 10,000 navvies and almost 1,000 horses, at times working on a 24-hour basis.*

No longer a county boundary, the Lune at least remains the limit of the Yorkshire Dales National Park, though no amount of persuasion can shake the author's inner conviction that the Yorkshire Dales end at the great watershed on Cam Fell, while Cumbria has yet to begin. This great intervening tract is noticeably different, neither Dales nor Lakeland, with its own unique appeal. This is Howgill country, Lune country, and for Dales Wayfarers, a peaceful interlude, a place for ambling along with the river rather than pressing on, a time to replenish batteries before the final scamper to Bowness, now not far away.

The bridge at the Crook of Lune is a graceful structure, a narrow packhorse bridge of old that today will pose problems to drivers of large modern cars. Fortunately, it rarely sees more than local traffic these days, and so the walk across it and up to the Lowgill viaduct (Ingleton-Tebay line) is usually a casual affair.

The road soon reaches a T-junction, and here the Way turns right for a short distance, and then left down the lane to Beck Foot. On reaching the first buildings turn left (PF sign) down a gravelled path with a small stream on the right, and looking very much as though you are entering someone's garden.

Continue in front of Half Island House to gain a slightly overgrown path at a gate. The path is stony underfoot, and follows a shallow groove along a field boundary, climbing easily until the boundary fence turns left. Here continue ahead (waymarked) along the line of an old field boundary, now with little more than a few hawthorns remaining, and at a prominent tree (waymark) bear half left to climb the pasture to its top corner. Cross a step stile and continue ahead along another old field boundary, with all the clammer that is the M6 motorway roaring by incessantly, augmented from time to time by the high speed passage of Inter City trains. Now, looking back, the Way starts to leave behind the sleek, rounded forms of the Howgills, and descends to a gate at the access to Lakethwaite Farm (607959).

Go left on the access track for a while until by a stile on the right just before the farm buildings a wide, sloping field can be gained. Head left, up the pasture, keeping buildings and enclosures on the left, and once beyond them continue climbing along the line of a semi-collapsed wall and hawthorn hedge ahead to a stile. The stile may not last much longer, and certainly the fence it once straddled has long since gone, leaving it an isolated and wholly useless relic. Now head for the top corner of the field, ignoring the tempting gate away to the right, and reach a waymarked stone stile giving on to an ancient highway.

Head left up the metalled roadway for about 80 metres to a public footpath sign at a stone step stile on the right. Cross the wall into the next field and follow its right hand wall to a gate; through the gate keep left with the wall until it is possible to descend slightly to reach a farm access bridge spanning the motorway.

Cross the motorway bridge and immediately turn sharp left on a public footpath (signposted: "Dales Way"); go through a gate to drop down behind a farmhouse on to a path leading to a step stile by which another metalled road may be gained. Head left along the road which widens for a short distance, and then narrows again. Just after it narrows look for a waymarked path dropping right to a gate. Now head half left to a gap stile, and from the stile head away along a shallow groove, and continue to a stone step stile. Ahead to a gate (waymarked), and along a drive to the right of the farm buildings at Holme Park.

Now ignore a waymarked path/stile on the right, but continue past the last building to another waymarked stile, giving on to a green path. Go right to pass through two successive gates, and then cross a field, dropping a little and aiming for a wall stile by a tree. Cross the next field, fence away to the left, and in the following field climb a small brow with a ruined building off to the right.

This slight eminence is a surprisingly good vantage point; the Howgills, and in particular Fell Head, remain for the moment prominent, but the central fells of Lakeland, its nearer eastern fringe, and the fells of Kentmere now start to draw attention away from the all-too-brief delights of the Lune Gorge.

Continue ahead now on to a path enclosed by two fences and leading up to Moresdale Hall. On passing the first buildings a small bridge is reached, with the access drive leading away to the left. Ignore the drive, and move slightly right after the bridge and climb half left up a slope to reach a higher and almost parallel driveway, with Moresdale Hall now in view on the right (588959).

Once more ignore the access road, cross it and continue ahead on an overgrown path through trees and rhododendrons. On leaving the copse, continue ahead with the left hand fence to cross a gully and small beck, and climb to a step stile in a wall. Turn left down a long lane, with a fine view across rolling countryside to the hamlet of Grayrigg, to a junction at Thatchmoor Head. Here, turn right and stroll down the lane to the first building on the right.

Just after the building, leave the lane by a gate on the left, and follow the top of a field, descending gradually to a white ladder stile giving on to the main railway line. Cross the line with all due care and attention, the trains along this stretch often approach at 100 mph. Enter the ensuing pasture and head directly away from the railway to descend between a small hillock on the left and the curve of a beck on the right, beyond which the Way reaches a Land Rover track leading to a gate (waymark). Ignore the gate, and continue instead left, with a tall hedge on the right, until the path becomes enclosed (and often muddy) between fences. Press on to a gate and turn right along another enclosed path leading to Green Head Farm.

Keep left of the farm buildings and descend the access track towards a cattle grid. Before the cattle grid turn right on a vague green path, leading to a gate and footbridge over a small beck near Grayrigg Foot. Aim for the gate near the farm and follow the drive out on to the A685. Turn right and head up the road for a short distance and then turn left along the access track to Thursgill Farm.

Long before Thursgill Farm is reached the track crosses a small beck, and here go left through a gate and cross the field to a stile. Now climb steeply and obliquely right, ignoring an obvious metal gate, but looking more to the right to locate a stile in a half concealed corner of the pasture. Continue ahead along the edge of pastureland, hawthorns on the left, to a track leading to a barn.

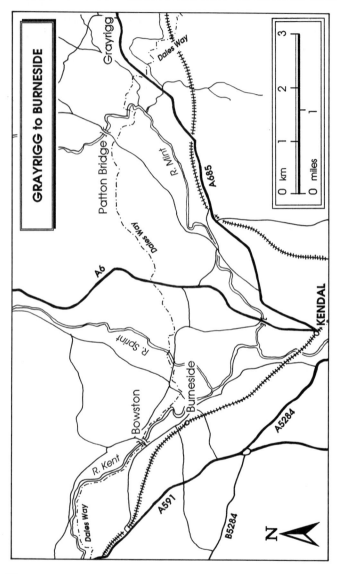

GRAYRIGG to BURNESIDE

Keep away from the barn, and go instead left through an iron gate and on to a narrow path across a field.

Throughout the whole of this delightful section there is a strong sense of isolation from civilisation, in spite of the numerous farms encountered en route. Walkers who enjoy solitude will find it here, and progress should be at the dead slow or stop end of the scale rather than at full speed ahead.

Continue ahead around a small knoll, and bear left to descend to a footbridge across the River Mint. Walk away from the footbridge, keeping to the right of a small group of trees, heading for a kissing gate giving on to an enclosed green lane, the old drive to the colonial-style mansion of Shaw End, which is followed up to the right. Continue with this lane for a while, and just after it starts descending look for another kissing gate on the left (waymarked), and here gain a parallel track through a field to a gate.

Beyond the gate follow a broad track, and when a building is reached on the left, leave the main track and turn left up a green track and through a white gate giving access to the garden of a private house, High Barn. Press on, quite legitimately in spite of the feeling of invading someone's privacy (which in any event we should respect), to reach an overgrown path at another white gate (waymarked).

A minor road is soon encountered and crossed, to descend the drive to Biglands. Pass in front of the buildings to a couple of stiles giving access to a long and narrow field, follow its right hand edge to a stile, in due course to gain a triangular shaped pasture leading by more stiles and obvious pathways to Black Moss Tarn.

On reaching the tarn go round its right hand edge, and climb to the intrusive electricity pylon, before descending directly to New House Farm. Enter the farm yard and go left of the house to a gate. Now an interesting path, once enclosed, runs away to meet the access road to Goodham Scales. Turn left, continue to a sharp bend left and here take a gate directly ahead (signposted: "Dales Way"). Now follow a track to the pleasant cluster of houses at Garnett Folds, reached at a gate, and continue down a narrow lane to meet the A6.

Go left a short distance along the A6 until a right turn leads up to Burton House. As you approach the farm, head for the gate to the left of the house, and then go immediately left through another gate before reaching one more giving access to an open and tilted pasture. There is a tempting gate to the right of this field leading on to a farm access track which will take you in the right direction, but it is not the rather less obvious recognised route. Instead head out across the field to a ladder stile at its far end, near a stretch of marshy ground, from where a short path leads through undergrowth to a narrow bridge across a beck, where the more obvious access track is encountered.

Now head up the field to go through a gate, and drop half left across a field to a stile in a corner. Climb to another directly above, and then follow the field boundary up a modest rise, across an intervening stile to descend to one in the bottom corner of the field on the left. Head directly away to a hedgerow, and go left to locate a stile where a drainage channel meets the field boundary. Gain the ensuing pasture and follow a hedgerow away, then through a gap, finally to reach a minor lane.

There are in fact two lanes here, that on the left going ahead directly to Burneside, while the Dales Way opts for the lesser road on the right, leaving it by a gate on the left just as the terraced row of Oakbank is reached. Follow the wall away and continue to the River Sprint, keeping left along its bank, past the bridge at Sprint Mill and continue to rejoin the road to Burneside.

4. Into Lakeland

The Dales Way turns away from Burneside, preferring not to enter the village, which is nevertheless a suitable place to spend what ought to be the last night before the end of the journey, or from which to catch a bus into Kendal. It will be found, too, that some of the proprietors of bed and breakfast accommodation in Burneside are quite willing to run Dales Wayfarers into Kendal, if necessary. (See "Accommodation Guide" for details.)

BURNESIDE

*The village of Burneside straddles the River Kent, and is sheltered on the north by Potter Fell, while **Burneside Hall**, a semi-fortified house with a pele tower dating to the fourteenth century, and built to keep marauding Scots at bay, lies on a raised tongue of land near the confluence of the rivers Kent and Sprint. Only a short distance from the larger town of Kendal, Burneside boasts a happy state of independence, and benefits from not having to cope with the Lakeland-bound traffic on the main road not too far away.*

Contrary to general belief, the name of Burneside does not derive from "burn" (there are no burns in the Lake District in the sense of brooks), but from the Norse "Bronolf's Head", and for centuries the manor was known as Burneshead; correctly it is pronounced Burn-e-side.

The manor was originally possessed by the de Burneshead family, the last of whom being Gilbert, whose daughter and heiress, Margaret, married Richard Bellingham of Tindale in Northumberland. During the reign of Edward II (1307-1327), the Bellinghams came to live at Burneshead and remained there until the middle of the sixteenth century. During that time Sir Henry Bellingham contrived to incur the displeasure of Edward IV (1461-1483) for having sided with the House of Lancaster, but it seems the family once more came into favour and managed to have its lands restored. Sir Roger Bellingham, Knight Banneret, was responsible for building Kendal church, where he was buried in 1533. It was his son, Sir Robert, who finally sold Burneside.

Later still, having been bought and sold three more times, Burneside

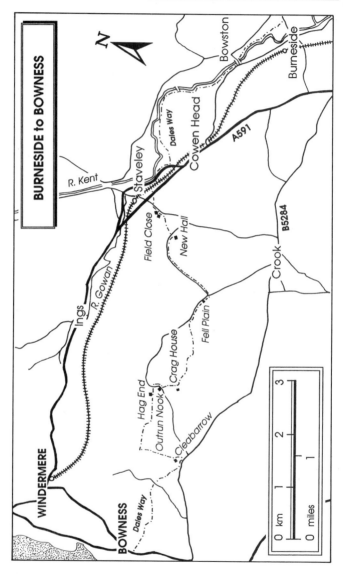

BURNESIDE to BOWNESS

came into the ownership of Richard Braithewaite of Ambleside, *popularly known as "Dapper Dick", who became Deputy Lieutenant of Westmorland and a justice of the peace until finally he moved to Yorkshire at the time of his second marriage, when he, too, sold the estate.*

The village now has been substantially enlarged by modern dwellings, while its prosperity hinges very much on that of its paper mill, an important source of employment.

✷ ✷ ✷

KENDAL

Kendal lies off the Dales Way, but it is a splendid town, famed as the birthplace of **Katherine Parr**, *the last of Henry VIIIs wives, and with much to offer Dales Way walkers.*

That Kendal has survived is something of a wonder, for it was on the receiving end of much of the attention of marauding Scots. In fact, it was the attempts of Kendalians to defend themselves that led to the building of Kendal's castle, and to its style of domestic building arrangement, common in Border country, with clusters of houses grouped around a yard and reached from the main highway by a gateway that could be securely bolted at night.

Kendal archers*, too, came to be renowned, as did the much-demanded* **"Kendal green"** *cloth produced by a process of dyeing and re-dyeing first in dyer's broom (Genista tinctoria), which was abundant in the Kent valley, and then blue woad. That Kendal cloth was much in demand can be seen from sixteenth century accounts held by the Cloth Hall as far away as Southampton where no less than 25 Kendal "chapmen" are recorded. Though no longer dependent on cloth manufacturing, Kendal's coat of arms not surprisingly bears the motto* pannus mihi panis - *wool is my bread.*

✷ ✷ ✷

BURNESIDE to STAVELEY
5 kilometres (3 miles)

Just before entering Burneside, leave the road, right, by a stile and kissing gate (PF signposted: "Bowston"). Follow a field boundary

to another kissing gate. Through the gate, then immediately right and left to follow a hedgerow left to a mill race. Either descend towards the water's edge following a path alongside a fence, or keep to the high ground, following the edge of pastureland, to descend to an iron ladder stile.

A field is then crossed to join the River Kent, which the Way accompanies upstream to steps leading on to Bowston Bridge. Cross the bridge and go up the lane to meet the road from Burneside. Keep right, along the road, until just after a telephone box on the left opposite Kent Close a narrow passageway (PF signposted: "Staveley" and "Dales Way") runs ahead obliquely on the right, between houses to rejoin the river, near a weir. Follow the lane in front of some houses, and then go along a narrow track on to the course of a former light railway which connected the mills at Cowen Head and Burneside with the Windermere branch line, shortly to join the road to Cowen Head. Continue past a telephone box to pass between two short rows of attractive cottages where the road ends, and a gate gives access once more to the Kent.

Now we follow the Kent on its true right bank, and keep on, passing a farm bridge (right) and attractive barn (left) to enter a pleasant wooded stretch with the Kent racing along merrily from its source way up on the High Street fells to Morecambe Bay.

The Kent is reputedly one of Britain's fastest flowing rivers, and its antics between Bowston and Staveley certainly support this claim. Walkers who stayed overnight at or near Burneside may be too preoccupied with thoughts of Bowness and Windermere to take in this brief encounter, the last with a river of any note, but our short acquaintance with it is quite delightful, worth appreciating, and Bowness really not so far away that haste is all important.

At one point the Way is forced away from the Kent by a pasture and wall. Cross the field to a distant stile, ignoring the waymarked gap on the right. Continue ahead across a wide open pasture to a wall with a stile on the left leading into a small plantation. Enter the woodland for a short distance, which avoids difficult going along the slippery, moss-covered riverbank, and exit by a stile into open meadow once more to follow the course of the river.

At a gap in a wall turn right, still following the river and at a second gap keep right following a wall between the path and the river until an enclosed track is reached, leading to Sandy Hill Farm. At a gate leave the farm access (a diversion effected in August 1991) and follow a clearly signposted route through a kissing gate. In the next field follow the wall around to another gate, turn right on an enclosed track to the main road into Staveley. Head right down the road towards Staveley.

STAVELEY

Until a new bypass brought much-needed and long-delayed relief, Staveley's greatest claim to fame was its reputation as a bottleneck for Lakeland traffic, which must have taken its toll on this tiny cluster of grey buildings. On the other hand, the opening of the bypass will have raised property values quite significantly.

The village sits neatly across the entrance to the Vale of Kentmere, at the confluence of the Rivers Kent and Gowan. This abundance of water was an important factor in the location of industry in rural areas during the nineteenth century. The production of wooden bobbins for the Lancashire mill industry, and the manufacture of gunpowder, depended not only on the ready availability of coppiced wood, but on the proximity of fast-flowing streams.

As a result there was a marked concentration of bobbin manufacturing mills along the Kent, particularly at Staveley where one company alone employed over 200 men and apprentices. By the 1870s however the industry was in decline; competition from abroad, notably Scandinavia, was an important factor, but it was to be the curtailment of child labour, on which the mills relied, under the Factory Act, 1867, which finally led to many mills closing down between 1867 and 1873.

✳ ✳ ✳

STAVELEY to BOWNESS
10.2 kilometres (6.25 miles)

The final stretch of any long walk is often greeted with an intoxicating mixture of relief and elation, a combination all the more enhanced if it passes through yet more splendid scenery, and especially if it leaves the view of journey's end until the last moment. As with the Pennine

Way, in this respect the Dales Way scores full marks, leading Wayfarers gradually through a terrain of grassy knolls, rocky hillocks, sweet green pastureland and flower-decked lanes and hedgerows, until suddenly and quite dramatically the end is in sight and all that remains is a downward plunge to the lake and Bowness with its busy cluster of shops, hotels, guest houses, restaurants and crowds of day visitors, none of whom will have the least understanding of your achievement.

The Way crosses the A591 into Staveley just south of the village, now a relatively tranquil retreat after the opening of the long awaited bypass. Take the signposted track (PF: "Dales Way") around Stock Bridge Farm to enter a walled lane leading to a railway underpass. A small stream bubbles along just over the wall, issuing from its own mini tunnel next to the underpass.

Once through the underpass three gates face you, the Way going right on to a broad green track enclosed by walls and delightful hedgerows of blackberry, beech and hawthorn. The left wall soon ends, becoming a neatly trimmed hedgerow, and here the path bears left, keeping to the edge of a pasture to another gate, with the white buildings of Moss Side ahead. Still following the wall continue to Moss Side, its buildings now modernised and providing a pleasant residential retreat.

As the first building is reached look for a waymarked stile (with a metal bar across it) taking the Way behind a garage to emerge into the forecourt of the buildings, from where the driveway leads on to the Crook road.

Now go left and cross the bypass, continuing to a slip road on the right leading to a signpost (PF: "Dales Way") and narrow lane to Field Close. Follow this and go left at the second building on a grass track to a gate, and ascend the ensuing field obliquely left to a kissing gate at the top. Here a small plantation is encountered, and the Way follows its edge (wall on the left) to another gate, climbing easily, and with a beautiful retrospective view across Staveley to Brunt Knott and the lower Kentmere fells.

On reaching the gate New Hall Farm springs into view, backed by the knolls of Carus Hill and Kerris Hill. Press on towards the farm on a rutted grassy track until an unfenced, metalled lane is reached, and here turn right. The lane, a narrow, quiet backroad flanked by wild flowers, rowan trees, young sycamore, beech, blackberries, bilberries and raspberries, passes through a couple of gates and climbs to the brow of a hill before a long descent to a T-junction near Fell Plain Farm.

The scenery in this tranquil region is typical of outer Lakeland, all part of its unique and magical appeal, a place of broad green pastures punctuated by rocky outcrops and dotted with small groups of trees. Yet here in this lost hinterland of Crook and Nether Staveley we could be in another world, a perfect, relaxing prelude to the grand finale, a last timeless corner in which to reflect on what has gone before.

Turn right to climb past Fell Plain Farm and the entrance to Glen Farm as far as a signposted green lane, left. Here leave the metalled lane and follow the lane, a bridleway enclosed by walls on both sides, rutted and flanked by gorse bushes. At its highest point there is a fine prospect, half right, of the Coniston Fells. Continue along the lane, descending now until it ends in a confrontation with a gate. A second gate just before it carries waymarks indicating the continuation of the Way. Pass through the gate and follow the wall left on a grassy path, bearing slightly away from it to a gap in a far wall near some small outcrops and a pile of stones. Here a better path appears and swings right to follow the edge of a small plantation of larches and blue spruce (not shown on the Outdoor Leisure Map).

As the end of the plantation is reached go left to parallel a small stream issuing from it. Do not cross the stream, but continue down to a gate, from where a pleasant path leads through an expanse of gorse bushes to a stile and a path following a wall (right) to Crag House Farm.

After having travelled for so long earlier in this journey in company with one of Britain's major rivers, it is interesting to encounter along the path to Crag House Farm what must be the briefest stretch of water, for here a stream issues energetically from its subterranean source only to disappear again within two metres. Where it comes from or goes to remains a mystery.

As the track reaches Crag House Farm leave it for a path, right, sandwiched between a small crag and a wall (signposted). A short climb leads to a gate. Follow the ensuing wall, pass between two trees and then swing left to a stile adjacent to Outrun Nook Farm.

Outrun Nook, now a dilapidated group of buildings, lies in a setting, to a mind with no responsibility for tending fields and flocks through the depths of winter in these hills, at once idyllic and full of romance. With the lack of perception only occasional visitors from towns and cities possess, we might wonder why so many of these old farms have reached the end of their days. Was it simply a question of economics, or of losing the constant battle against the elements? Or did something long since forgotten finally turn the finger of fate against those who struggled to eke a living from the hills? Such sights are sad to see, but remain a poignant reminder, if we care to reflect for a while, of times gone by when all the trappings of modern life we now take for granted were just so much pie in the sky.

Leave Outrun Nook to its quiet decay, and follow the lane, right, for a while to a signposted track leading to Hag End Farm. This farm, too, use to be uninhabited, but was once more occupied during the preparation of this guide, and the last resting place, or so it seems, of a collection of Range Rovers and old farm vehicles.

Only a few miles to go: Lakeland fells form the distant skyline for the first time

At Hag End look for a small sign to the left of the buildings, and follow an obscure path into a rough pasture beyond, climbing to a stone step stile. On a narrow path continue easily across rough fell pasture on a green path, improving as it approaches a gap in a partially collapsed wall.

Beyond the gap continue through more pasture on a green path to its highest point where there opens up a magnificent panorama of the Lakeland mountains from Black Combe far away to the left, across the Coniston Fells, Crinkle Crags and Bowfell, with the dark shapes of the Scafells between them, and on to the Langdale Pikes, the Fairfield group, Red Screes, Stony Cove Pike and the Kentmere Fells.

Continue down now to a gate beneath the outcrop of School Knott. Go left through the gate to another gate, and then join a broad track crossed a short way further on by a small stream. This track soon leads away, right, to Windermere town, while the Dales Way leaves it, left, by a narrow (and not too obvious) path descending to a farm track. Here the stream forded a few moments ago is encountered once more and this time crossed by a slab of rock.

A broad, metalled track now leads through High Cleabarrow to join the B5284 for a desperate 150 metres (right) of self-preservation until the Way escapes the road by a signposted track (letterbox nearby) leading to Low Cleabarrow. Just before reaching a group of farm buildings, turn left on a signposted track to a gate, and then follow a field along its right edge with a wall to first one and then two more gates in quick succession either side of a large oak tree. Now climb a little to a waymark post and continue ahead into stands of oak, two of which are marked by white arrows, and on to a gate with a small stream nearby.

Climb once more to a gate at a minor road. Cross the road to a gate and bear left in the ensuing field to a farm access track at another gate. The way ahead is obvious, leading to a kissing gate in a wall near the edge of a plantation. Keep beneath the edge of the plantation on a good path until it swings left on to a metalled lane. Turn right along the lane for a few metres, and leave it, left, by a narrow path with an iron fence on the left and young oak trees on the right. Ahead now to a wrought iron gate,

The end of the journey: Bowness, a stark contrast to much of what has gone before

and a pleasant traverse of pastureland beyond. Another iron gate at the top of the field gives access to the next pasture, where the Way follows the edge of the field to a walled track leading to a road at the entrance to Birkdale Farm. Continue ahead across the road on to another walled path to a gate.

Only now as we reach this gate does Windermere at long last spring into view, and suddenly the end is drawing us on, downhill.

Continue around the right edge of meadowland with beautiful stands of oak trees, and tantalising glimpses of Windermere and Belle Isle ahead, shimmering above the rooftops of Bowness.

Descend to two kissing gates across a track leading right to Bowness and left to Post Knott. The Dales Way in its final downward flight continues ahead. Now Windermere really opens up, a magnificent view and splendid reward. Thoughtfully a slab of Lakeland slate has been positioned just to the right of the track here "For those who walk the Dales Way". Continue down, steeply, to reach the first of the houses of Bowness at Brant Fell Road. The road leads straight into the heart of Bowness, reaching the hubbub of day trippers at the

Spinnery Restaurant, reputedly the oldest building in Bowness, and thought to be some 400 years old.

Press on ahead to join the road down to the lake for a ceremonial dipping of the boots in the water to mark the end.

WELL DONE!

Conclusion

The completion of any long walk in a day and age when soft options are so readily available is no mean achievement. And really it matters not whether the walk was 80 miles or 800, whether you did it all in one go or gradually over a period of weeks or months. It is the triumph of personal determination and commitment that is all important, for on these two virtues rests the whole architecture of our lives. With 78 miles of riverside walking, dales, wild moorland, high mountains and open countryside behind you, the Dales Way will come to be an experience that will last a lifetime.

BIBLIOGRAPHY

Companion into Lakeland, Maxwell Fraser (Methuen & Co., 1937)
Dales Way Companion, Paul Hannon (Hillside Publications, 1988)
A History of Cumberland and Westmorland, William Rollinson (Phillimore & Co., 1978)
The Lake Counties, W.G. Collingwood (J.M. Dent & Sons Ltd, 1902)
On Foot in Yorkshire, Donald Boyd (Alexander Maclehose & Co., 1932)
Parish and People of the Yorkshire Dales through Ten Centuries, Susan D. Brooks (1973)
The Pennine Mountains, Terry Marsh (Hodder and Stoughton, 1989)
Pennine Panorama, Peter Wightman (Gerrard, Nelson, 1969)
Portrait of Yorkshire, Harry J. Scott (Robert Hale, 1965)
Striding through Yorkshire, Alfred J. Brown (Country Life Ltd, 1938)
Upper Wharfedale, F.W. Houghton (Dalesman Books, 1980)
Wharfedale, Ella Pontefract and Marie Hartley (J.M. Dent and Sons Ltd, 1938)
The Yorkshire Pennines of the North West, W. Riley (Herbert Jenkins Ltd, 1934)
Yorkshire: The Dales, Maurice Colbeck (B.T. Batsford Ltd, 1979)
Yorkshire through the years, Ian Dewhirst (B.T. Batsford Ltd, 1975)
Yorkshire Villages, G. Bernard Wood (Robert Hale, 1971)
Yorkshire: West Riding, Arthur Mee, ed. (Hodder and Stoughton, 1941)

THE DALES WAY

Accommodation Guide

ACCOMMODATION GUIDE

This Accommodation Guide, compiled in January 1992, is intended to be updated annually. Walkers with information to add to the guide, or comments about any of the accommodation services mentioned, should contact the author through the publisher. Such comments would be much appreciated and, where appropriate, treated in confidence.

The list of accommodation is not exhaustive, and is the product of a preliminary trawl of bed and breakfast, etc. facilities carried out at the end of 1991. Walkers should check the tariffs for 1992 and subsequent years directly with the proprietor.

YOUTH HOSTELS
The following youth hostels are on or near the Dales Way. Full details of their opening times should be checked with the YHA Accommodation Guide and/or the Yorkshire Area Office, 96 Main Street, Bingley, West Yorkshire, BD16 2JH (0274 567697)

LINTON (GR 998627): The Old Rectory, Linton-in-Craven, Skipton, North Yorkshire, BD23 5HH (0756 752400)
KETTLEWELL (GR 970724): Whernside House, Kettlewell, Skipton, North Yorkshire, BD23 5QU (0756 760232)
DENTDALE (GR 773850):Cowgill, Dent, Sedbergh, Cumbria, LA10 5RN (05875 251)
KENDAL: Highgate, Kendal, Cumbria, LA9 4HE (0539 724066)
WINDERMERE (GR 405013): High Cross, Bridge Lane, Troutbeck, Windermere, Cumbria, LS23 1LA (05394 43543)

CAMP SITES
There are few established camp sites along the Dales Way, though many farmers will allow the odd tent or two. To help preserve good relations with farmers, please make a point of obtaining permission before camping.

114

Wharfedale

Information may be obtained from the Ilkley Tourist Information Office, Station Road, Ilkley (0943 602319), about camping in and around Ilkley. Other sites include:

Howgill Lodge, BARDEN, Skipton, North Yorkshire, BD23 6DJ (GR 064592) (0756 720655)

Mill Lane, APPLETREEWICK, Skipton, North Yorkshire, BD23 6DD (GR 040601) (0756 720275/720236)

Wood Nook, Skirethorns, THRESHFIELD, Skipton, North Yorkshire, BD23 5NU (GR 972641) (0756 752412)

Fold Farm, KETTLEWELL, Skipton, North Yorkshire, BD23 5RJ (GR 975725) (0756 760886)

Beckermonds East Farm, BUCKDEN, Skipton, North Yorkshire, (0756 760816)

Dentdale

Harbergill Farm, COWGILL, Dent, Sedbergh, Cumbria, LA10 5RG (GR 764868) (05875 392)

Ewegales Farm, DENT, Sedbergh, Cumbria, LA10 5RH (GR 755867) (05875 440)

Conder Farm, DENT, Sedbergh, Cumbria (GR 706867) (05875 277)

High Laning Farm, DENT, Sedbergh, Cumbria, LA10 5QJ (GR 703870) (05875 239)

Barrett Farm, SEDBERGH, Cumbria (GR 648916)

Lincoln's Inn Farm, Bridge End, SEDBERGH, Cumbria (05396 20567)

Pinfold Caravan Park, Garsdale Road, SEDBERGH, Cumbria, LA10 5JL (GR 665920) (05396 20576)

Barn Farm, CROOK, Cumbria (GR 479956)

BUNKHOUSE BARNS

The provision of bunkhouse barns is the result of an initiative between the Countryside Commission and the Yorkshire Dales National Park authority, and aims to provide simple, inexpensive overnight accommodation. With the commendable notion of reclaiming otherwise redundant barns, these "bunkhouses" offer basic accommodation, toilet (including shower), cooking facilities, an eating area and a drying room. Self-catering facilities include the provision of cutlery and crockery, while dairy produce may often be obtained close by, particularly if ordered in advance. Sleeping bags may also be hired. Bookings should be made direct, and advance booking is preferred. The bunkhouse barns are at present just a little too few on the ground to allow the Dales Way to be completed in its entirety using barns, though strong walkers could manage it.

BARDEN TOWER (GR 050572) Mr I.H. Leak, High Gamsworth Cottage, Barden, Skipton, North Yorkshire, BD23 6DH (0756 720630)
HUBBERHOLME (GR 929780) Mrs A. Falshaw, Grange Farm, Hubberholme, Skipton, North Yorkshire, BD23 5JE (0756 760259)
OUGHTERSHAW (GR 868815) Mrs S.V. Bentley, Hazel Bank Farm, Oughtershaw, Skipton, North Yorkshire, BD23 5JR (0756 760312)
CAM (GR 824822) Mrs Dorothy Smith, Cam Farm, Oughtershaw, Skipton, North Yorkshire, BD23 5JT (0860 648045)
CATHOLES (GR 653908) Mrs J. Handley, Catholes Farm, Sedbergh, Cumbria, LA10 5SS (05396 20334)

BED AND BREAKFAST ACCOMMODATION
The following is a selection of accommodation available, based on information supplied by the proprietors. Please note, an evening meal is not always available (and should in any case always be booked in advance). The list does indicate those proprietors who have indicated a willingness to provide evening meals; the absence of such an indication should not, however, deter you from asking.

KEY
PH = Private house, bungalow or cottage; GH = Guest House; H = Hotel; I = Inn; F = Farmhouse; D = No. of double rooms; T = No. of twins; F = No. of family rooms; S = No. of singles; EM = Evening meal provided

ADDINGHAM, West Yorkshire. Tel. Code 0943
1. Mrs A. Gill, West Hall, Nesfield (830573): PH: D1 T/F1 S1: EM
2. Mrs Goodwin, 27 Wharfe Park, LS29 0QZ (831370): PH: D1 T1 S1: EM
3. Mrs Pauline Pape, Olicana Cottage, High Mill Lane, LS29 0RD (830500): PH: D1 T1

4. Mrs M. Windle, 69a Main Street, LS29 0PD (831040): PH: T1

APPLETREEWICK, Skipton, North Yorkshire. Tel. Code 0756
5. Mrs Eileen Baron, Haugh Side, BD23 6DQ (720225): PH: D1 T1 S1: EM
6. Mrs Alyson Coney, Blundellstead, BD23 6DB (720632): PH: D1 S2
(Dogs welcome; drying facilities)
7. Mr John Pitchers, The New Inn, BD23 6DA (720252): I: D1 T2 S1

BARDEN, Bolton Abbey, Skipton, North Yorkshire.
Tel. Code: 0756
8. Mrs A. Foster, Howgill Lodge, BD23 6DJ (720655): PH: D2 T1 F1:
Early EM
9. Mrs Dorothy Parkinson, Holme House Farm BD23 6AT (720661):
F: D1 T1

BEAMSLEY, Bolton Abbey, Skipton, North Yorkshire.
Tel. Code 0756
10. Mrs Gwen Grange, Ling Chapel Farm, Langbar Road, BD23 6HR
(710226): F: D1 T1: EM

BOLTON ABBEY, Skipton, North Yorkshire. Tel. Code 0756
11. Mrs C. Crabtree, Bolton Park Farm, BD23 6AW (710244): F: D1
T1 F1
12. Mr Martin C.G. Harris, Devonshire Arms Country House Hotel,
BD23 6AJ (710441): H: D18 T21 F1: EM

BOWNESS-ON-WINDERMERE, Cumbria. Tel. Code 05394
13. Miss Jennifer Bailey, Nagoya Country House, 4 Brackenfield
(44356): GH: D2 T1
14. Mr and Mrs Jim and Jan Bebbington, Holly Cottages, Rayrigg
Road, LA23 3BZ (44250): GH: D5 T1 F2
15. Mr and Mrs Martin and Sandra Britton, Virginia Cottage, Kendal
Road, LA23 3EJ (44891): GH: D9 F2
16. Mrs Mary Bunker, Laurel Cottage, St Martin's Square, LA23 3EF
(45594): PH: D12 T3 F2 S2
17. Miss C.H. Furneaux, Lyndhurst, 101 Craig Walk, LA23 2JF
(44304): PH: D1 F1 S1
18. Mr and Mrs Brian and Valerie Garvey, Field House, Belsfield
Terrace, LA23 3EQ (42476): GH: D5 T3 F3

19. Mr Peter Granger, Holmlea, Kendal Road, LA23 3EW (42597): GH: D3 T1 F1 S2

20. Mr Neil Grantham, Belsfield Guest House, 4 Belsfield Terrace, LA23 3EQ (45823): GH: D5 T/F4

21. Mr Raymond A. Gregory, St John's Lodge, LA23 2EQ (43078): H: D10 T3 F1 S1: EM

22. Mr and Mrs Brian and Margaret Hodgkinson, Elim Bank Hotel, Lake Road, LA23 2JJ (44810): H: D3 F5 S1: EM

23. Mrs Pauline Holland, Brooklands, Ferry View, LA23 3JB (42344): GH: D1 T1 F3 S1

24. Mrs Rachel Jamieson, Robin's Nest, 1 North Terrace, LA23 3AU (46446): PH: D2 T/F2 (Singles available at quiet times)

25. Mrs Susan Lewthwaite, Beech Tops, Meadowcroft Lane, Storrs Park, LA23 3JJ (45453): GH: D1 F1

26. Mrs J.E. Pert, Brook House, 3 Craig Walk, LA23 2ES (43809): PH: D2 S2: EM (if pre-booked)(No Smoking)

27. Mrs Janet E. Poole, Beechwood Private Hotel, Beresford Road, LA23 2JG (43403): GH: D4 T2 F1

28. Mr and Mrs Riggs, The Poplars, Lake Road, LA23 2EQ (42325): GH: D4 T/F2 S1: EM

29. Mrs Vicky Robinson, White Lodge Hotel (43624): H: D6 T/F3 S3: EM

30. Mr and Mrs Dave and Val Rumbles, Fell View Guest House, 38 Craig Walk, LA23 2JT (45596): GH: D3 T1 F1

31. Mrs Kathleen M. Shankley, 77 Craig Walk, LA23 2JT (43542): GH: D2 S1

32. Mrs Celia Stevenson, New Hall Bank, Fallbarrow Road, LA23 3DJ (43558): GH: D7 T1 F4 S2

33. Mr and Mrs Philip and Marilyn Tordoff, Langdale View Guest House, 114 Craig Walk (off Helm Road), LA23 3AX (44076): GH: D3 T2 S1: EM

34. Mrs Joyce Whitfield, Eastbourne Hotel, Biskey Howe Road, LA23 2JR (43525): H: D4 F2 S2: EM (between October and May)

35. Mr and Mrs D. and N. Willis-Utting, Bay House Lake View Guest House, Fallbarrow Road, LA23 3DJ (43383): GH: D3 T1 F2: EM

BUCKDEN, North Yorkshire. Tel. Code 0756

36. Mr Nigel Hayten, The Buck Inn, BD23 5JA (760228): I: D5 T3 F2 S2: EM

37. Mr and Mrs J. Leach, Ghyll Cottage, BD23 5JA (760340): PH: D1 T1

38. Ms Lynn Thornborrow, West Winds Cottage, BD23 5JA (760883): PH: D2 T1

BURNESIDE, Kendal, Cumbria. Tel. Code 0539
39. Mrs S. Beaty, Garnett House Farm, LA9 5SF (724542): F: D1 T1 F2: EM
40. Mrs A. Eleanor Bell, Hillfold Farm, LA8 9AU (722574): F: D/T/F3: EM
41. Mrs J. Ellis, Gateside Farm, LA9 5SE (722036): F: D3 T1 F1: EM
42. Mrs June Mitchell, Hill Farm, Garnett Bridge Road, LA9 9AU (741273): F: D1 F1: Simple EM, or will provide free lift to local pub

BURNSALL, Skipton, North Yorkshire. Tel Code: 0756
43. Mr J. Cobbett, Fell Hotel, BD23 6BT (720209): H: D9 T2 F2: EM
44. Mr W.T. Haighton, Manor House Hotel, BD23 6BW (720231): H: D4 T3 F1 (S supplement): EM
45. Mrs Anita Hall, Holly Tree Farm, Thorpe, BD23 6BJ (720604): F: D1 S1
46. Mrs Ann Mason, Conistone House, BD23 6BN (720650): PH: D1 T2
47. Mrs J.M. Wallace, The Green, BD23 6BS (720210): PH: D2: EM
48. Mr and Mrs L. and P.S. Warnett, Red Lion Hotel, BD23 6BU (720204): H: D7 T3 F1 S1: EM

CONISTONE-WITH-KILNSEY, North Yorkshire. Tel. Code 0756
49. Mrs Vanessa Roberts, Mossdale, BD23 5HS (752320): F: T3

DENTDALE, Cumbria. Tel. Code 05875
Cowgill
50. Mrs Margaret Clark, Birk Rigg Guest House, Cowgill, LA10 5RN (367): GH: D1 T1 F1
51. Mrs Mary Ferguson, Scow Cottage, Cowgill, LA10 5RN (445): PH: D1 T1
52. Mr and Mrs Ron and Sandra Martin, The Sportsman Inn, Cowgill, LA10 5RG (282): I: D3 T2 F1 (S only if available, not weekends) EM: (Dogs welcome, by prior arrangement)
53. Mrs M.M. Parkes, Carley Hall Cottages, Cowgill LA10 5RL (244): F: D1 T1: EM

Dent

54. Mrs Gwynneth Cheetham, Smithy Fold, LA10 5RE (368): PH: D1 T1 F1

55. Mrs Dorothy Goad, The George and Dragon, Main Street, LA10 5QL (256): H: D4 T4 F2: EM

56. Mr G. Hudson, Stone Close Tea Shop and Guest House, Main Street, Dent, LA10 5QL (231): GH: D1 F1 S1: EM

57. Mrs Christine Oversby, Low Hall, Dent (232): F: D2 S1

58. Mr and Mrs E. Smith, Garda View Guest House, LA10 5QL (209): GH: D2 T1

59. Mr Martin Stafford, The Sun Inn, Main Street, LA10 5QL (208): I: D1 T1 F1: EM

Gawthrop

60. Mrs Eileen Gardner, Bridge Cottage, Gawthrop, LA10 5TA (240): PH: D1 T1 F1: EM

GRASSINGTON, Skipton, North Yorkshire. Tel. Code: 0756
Grassington

61. Mr and Mrs N. Benson, Raines Close Guest House, 13 Station Road, BD23 5LS (752678): GH: D3 T1

62. Mrs P. Berry, Springroyd House, 8a Station Road, BD23 5NQ (752473): PH: D1 T1

63. Mrs Cullingford, Craven Cottage, Main Street, BD23 5AA (752205): GH: D2 F1

64. Mr R.G. Davey, The Black Horse Hotel, Garrs Lane, BD23 5AT (752770): H: D10 T3 F1: EM

65. Mr and Mrs Gordon and Linda Elsworth, Grassington House Hotel, BD23 5AQ (752406): H: D6 T2 S2: EM

66. Mr and Mrs Linda and Keith Harrison, Ashfield House, BD23 5AE (752584): H: D4 T3: EM

67. Mr and Mrs J. and B. Lingard, The Lodge, 8 Wood Lane, BD23 5LU (752518): GH: D4 T4 F1: EM

68. Mrs Marian Lister, Town Head Guest House, 1 Low Lane, BD23 5AU (752811): GH: D4 T1: EM

69. Mr D. Lockyer, Kirkfield, BD23 5LJ (752385): GH: D1 T1 F2: EM

70. Mr and Mrs K.J. Marsden, Burtree Cottage, Hebden Road, BD23 5LH (752442): PH: D1 T1 (No Smoking)

71. Mr and Mrs David and Shirley Paling, Brown Fold Cottage, off Main Street, BD23 5AB (752314/752416): PH: D1 T1

72. Mrs Rita M. Richardson, The Foresters Arms, BD23 5AA (752349): I: D4 T1 F2: EM

73. Mr and Mrs J.H. Thompson, Chapel Fold Guest House, BD23 5BG (752075): GH: D2 T1: EM

Threshfield

74. Mr John Ball, 2 Woodland View, Threshfield, BD23 5NA (753166): PH: D1 T1 S1

75. Mrs Norma Cahill, Franor House, 3 Wharfeside Avenue, Threshfield, BD23 5BS (752115): PH: D/F1 T1 S1

76. Mrs Sheila Carr, Farfield, Wharfeside Avenue, Threshfield, BD23 5BS (752435): PH: T1 F1 S1

77. Mrs Janette Kitching, Grisedale Farm, Threshfield, BD23 5NT (752516): F: D1 T1 F1

78. Mrs Josil Pope, 7 Badger Gate, Threshfield, BD23 5ES (753114): PH: T1

79. Mr and Mrs J.K. Ramsden, Craiglands, Threshfield, BD23 5ER (752093): PH: D1 T1 S2

80. Mr and Mrs Allan and Eileen Thompson, Bridge End Farm, Threshfield, BD23 5NH (752463): F: D2 T1 F1: EM

GRAYRIGG, Cumbria. Tel. Code: 053984

81. Mrs Jean Bindloss, Grayrigg Hall, LA8 9BU (689): PH: D1 F1: EM

82. Mrs D. Johnson, Grey Gables, LA8 9BU (345): PH: D2 T1: EM

83. Mrs Anne Knowles, Myers Farm, Docker, LA8 0DF (610): F: D1 F1: EM

HEBDEN, North Yorkshire. Tel. Code: 0756

84. Mr and Mrs K. and C. Lakin, Clarendon Hotel, BD23 5DE (752446): H: D2 T1: EM

HUBBERHOLME, Skipton, North Yorkshire. Tel. Code: 0756

85. Mrs A. Falshaw, Grange Farm, BD23 5JE (760259): PH: D1 T1

86. Mr John Fredrick, The George Inn, Kirk Gill, BD23 5JE (760223) I: D2 T2: EM

87. Mrs A. Huck, Church Farm, BD23 5JE (760240): F: D1 F1

88. Mrs S.M. Middleton, Low Raisgill Cottage, Raisgill, BD23 5JQ (760351): PH: D1 T1: EM
89. Mrs Lynda Robinson, Kirkgill Manor Guest House, BD23 5JE (760800) GH: D4 T1 F1: EM

ILKLEY, West Yorkshire. Tel. Code: 0943
90. Mrs Barbara L. Battey, Belmont, Queens Road, LS29 9QL (602445): PH: D2 T1 S3: EM
91. Mrs Pat Bradbury, 1 Tivoli Place (609483): PH: D1 T2 F1: EM
92. Mr and Mrs Alfred and Pat Below, Archway Cottage, 24 Skipton Road, LS29 9EP (603399): PH: D2 T2: EM
93. Mrs Audrey Coleman, 6 Woodlands Rise, Grove Park (608889): PH: D1
94. Mrs Kristine Dobson, Riverside Hotel, Bridge Lane (607338): H: D4 T3 F3 S2: EM
95. Mr Norman Emslie, The Grove Hotel, 66 The Grove (600298): H: T2 F2 S1: EM
96. Mrs A. Fidler, Beech House, 5 St James Road, LS29 9PY (601995): PH: D1 T1 S1: EM
97. Mrs Stella Kemp, Daleside, 12 Manley Road (602962): PH: D1 T1 S1
98. Mrs Carol Minto, Briarwood, 20 Queens Drive, LS29 9QW: PH: D1 T1: EM
99. Mrs Y. O'Neill, 8 Bolton Bridge Road (608436): PH: T1 F1
100. Mrs Stella M. Read, 126 Skipton Road (600635): PH: T1
101. Mrs Vera Scaife, 19 River View, Leeds Road (601261): PH: D1 T1
102. Mrs Betty Taylor, Hollygarth House, 293 Leeds Road (609223): PH: D1 T1 F2 S1
103. Mrs J. Terry, Belvedere, 2 Victoria Avenue (607598): PH: D1 T1 F1 S1: (Sandwiches and packed lunches available; flasks filled)
104. Mr R.A. Voss, Summerhill Guest House, 24 Crossbeck Road (607067): GH: D1 T5 S1: EM
105. Mrs Janine Withrington, Rose and Crown Hotel, Church Street (607260): H: D3 T1 F1

KENDAL, Cumbria. Tel. Code 0539
106. Mrs Marilyn Baines, Beech House, 40 Greenside, LA9 4LD (720385): GH: D3 T3 F2 (Rooms let as singles when quiet): EM
107. Mrs Cathryn Bigland, Brantholme, 7 Sedbergh Road, LA9 6AD (722340): GH: T3: EM

108. Mrs Sheila Brindley, Bridge House, 65 Castle Street, LA9 7AD (722941): GH: D1 T1 S1 (Drying facilities; packed lunches)(NOTE: Will collect and deliver walkers to and from the Dales Way)

109. Mrs Brenda Denison, Hillside Guest House, 4 Beast Banks, LA9 4JW (722836): GH: D3 T1 S2

110. Mrs Doreen Dixon, Mereside, 58 Shap Road, LA9 6DP (727703): PH: D1 T1 S1

111. Mrs Sylvia Fitzgerald, Springwell House, 133 Windermere Road, LA9 5EP (722958): GH: D1 T1

112. Mrs J. Grimshaw, Meadow Bank, Shap Road, LA9 6NY (721926): PH: D1 T3 F1 S1

113. Mrs Gillian Kellington, Welton Rise, 44 Shap Road, LA9 6DP (732464): PH: D1 T1 F1 S1

114. Mrs M. Paylor, Fairways Guest House, 102 Windermere Road, LA9 5EZ (725564): GH: D3 F1 S1

115. Mrs Elsie M. Walker, Fernlea Guest House, 46 Shap Road, LA9 6DP (720402): GH: D1 T2 F2 S2

116. Mr and Mrs Arthur and Helen Welch, Rainbow Hotel, 32 Highgate, LA9 4SX (724178/728271): H: D5 T2 F2 S1

117. Mr David Young, Kentdale Brow, 19 Serpentine Road, LA9 4PF (722591): PH: T1 F1

KETTLEWELL, Skipton, North Yorkshire. Tel. Code 0756
118. Miss Sally Brown, The King's Head, BD23 5RD (760242): I: D3 T2 F1 S1: EM

119. Mr Anthony Butterfield, Dale House, BD23 5QZ (760836): H: D6 T2: EM

120. Mr Timothy Earnshaw, Langcliffe House, BD23 5RJ (760243): GH: D2 T3 S2: EM

121. Mrs Barbara Lambert, Fold Farm, BD23 5RJ (760886): F: D2 T1

122. Miss M.A. Lister, Cam Lodge, BD23 5QU (760276): F: D1 T2: EM

123. Mrs Lorna Thornborrow, Lynburn, BD23 5RF (760803): PH: D1 T1

LINTON, Skipton, North Yorkshire. Tel. Code 0756
124. Mrs P.S. Metcalfe, Grange Cottage, BD23 5HH (752527): PH: D1 T1

125. Mr and Mrs Brian and Mary Sutcliffe, Langerton House Farm, BD23 5HN (730260): F: D1 F1

LUNEDALE, Kendal, Cumbria. Tel. Code 053984
126. Mrs D. Hogg, Tarnclose, Beckfoot, Lowgill, LA8 0BL (658): PH:
D1 T1 S1: EM

OUGHTERSHAW, Skipton, North Yorkshire. Tel. Code 0860
127. Mrs Dorothy Smith, Cam Houses, BD23 5JT (648045): FH: T2:
EM and refreshments available (See also under entry for Bunkhouse
Accommodation)

RIBBLEHEAD, North Yorkshire. Tel. Code 0468
128. Mrs Eileen Beresford, Newby Head Farm, Hawes, DL8 3LX
(Code: 05875 347): F: D1 F1: EM
129. Mrs Doreen Timmins, Gearstones Farm, LA6 3AS (41405): F: T1
F1: EM

SEDBERGH, Cumbria. Tel. Code 05396
130. Mrs Janet C. Baines, 19 Bainbridge Road, LA10 5AU (20638):
PH: D1 T1 S1
131. Mr and Mrs B. and I. Garnett, Dalesman Country Inn, Main
Street, LA10 5BN (21183): I: D1 T2 F3: EM
132. Mrs Marjorie C. Hoggarth, The Myers, Joss Lane, LA10 5AS
(20257): PH: D1 T1 S1
133. Mrs Anne E. Hunter, Rash House, Dentfoot, LA10 5SU (20113):
PH: D1 F1: EM (on request, when booking)
134. Mrs Jill Jarvis, The Moss, Garsdale Road, LA10 5JL (20940): PH:
D2 T1: EM
135. Mrs Patricia Kerry, Marshall House, Main Street, LA10 5BL
(21053): PH: D1 T2 (Drying room available)
136. Mr and Mrs D. and E. Liddey-Smith, Turvey House, 1 The
Leyes, LA10 5DJ (20841): GH: D1 T1 F1
137. Mrs Elsie Mattinson, Ash-Hining Farm, Howgill, LA10 5HU
(20957): F: D1 T1
138. Mrs Pat Ramsden, Sun Lea, Joss Lane, LA10 5AS (20828): PH:
D2 T1
139. Mrs Susan Sharrocks, Holmecroft, Station Road, LA10 5DW
(20754): GH: D2 T1
140. Mrs Margaret R. Swainbank, 25 Bainbridge Road, LA10 5AU
(20685): PH: D1 T/F1 S1

141. Mrs Joan Snow, Randall Hall, Station Road, LA10 5HJ (20633): PH: D1 T2
142. Miss M. Thurlby, 15 Back Lane, LA10 5AQ (20251): PH: D1 T1 (Dogs welcome)
143. Mr Harry Wilkinson, The Bull Hotel, Main Street, LA10 5BL (20264): H: D6 T3 F3 S2: EM

SKELMSMERGH, Cumbria. Tel. Code 053983
144. Mrs Josephine Barnett, Thorneyslack Farm, Garth Row, LA8 9AW (657): F: D1 T1 (No Smoking)
145. Mrs Helen Metcalfe, Hollin Root Farm, Garth Row, LA8 9AW (638): F: D1 T1 F1 S1: Light meals available

STARBOTTON, Skipton, North Yorkshire. Tel. Code 0756
146. Mr and Mrs B.T. Rathmell, Hilltop, BD23 5HY (760321): GH: D3 T1 F1: EM

STAVELEY, Cumbria. Tel. Code 0539
147. Mr Hamish Alexander, Danes House, 1 Danes Road, LA8 9PW (821294): PH: F2
148. Mrs Sandra Barlow, Hill View, Kentmere Road, LA8 9JF (821494): PH: D2 F1
149. Mr and Mrs Paul and Honor Brind, Burrow Hall Country Guest House, Plantation Bridge, LA8 9JR (821711): GH: D1 T2: EM
150. Mrs Betty Fishwick, Stock Bridge Farm, Kendal Road, LA8 9LP (821580): F: D4 F1 S1
151. Mr and Mrs David and Phyllis Kelly, Fell View, 12a Danes Road, LA8 9PW (821209): GH: D1 T1 F1 S1

YOCKENTHWAITE, Buckden, Skipton, North Yorkshire. Tel. Code 0756
152. Mrs Elizabeth Hird, Yockenthwaite, BD23 5JH (760835): F: D1 T1 S1 (No Evening Meals, but will ferry guests to George Inn at Hubberholme or to Buckden).

CICERONE GUIDES - EUROPE

Cicerone publish a wide range of reliable guides to walking and climbing in Europe, as well as a large selection of guides to Britain

FRANCE
TOUR OF MONT BLANC
CHAMONIX MONT BLANC - A Walking Guide
TOUR OF THE OISANS: GR54
WALKING THE FRENCH ALPS: GR5
THE CORSICAN HIGH LEVEL ROUTE: GR20
THE WAY OF ST JAMES: GR65
THE PYRENEAN TRAIL: GR10
TOUR OF THE QUEYRAS
ROCK CLIMBS IN THE VERDON
THE ROBERT LOUIS STEVENSON TRAIL
WALKS IN VOLCANO COUNTRY

FRANCE / SPAIN
WALKS AND CLIMBS IN THE PYRENEES
ROCK CLIMBS IN THE PYRENEES

SPAIN
WALKS & CLIMBS IN THE PICOS DE EUROPA
WALKING IN MALLORCA
BIRDWATCHING IN MALLORCA
COSTA BLANCA CLIMBS

FRANCE / SWITZERLAND
THE JURA - Walking the High Route and
 Winter Ski Traverses

SWITZERLAND
THE ALPINE PASS ROUTE
WALKS IN THE ENGADINE
THE BERNESE ALPS - A Walking Guide
WALKING IN TICINO
THE VALAIS - A Walking Guide

GERMANY / AUSTRIA
THE KALKALPEN TRAVERSE
KLETTERSTEIG - Scrambles
WALKING IN THE BLACK FOREST
MOUNTAIN WALKING IN AUSTRIA
WALKING IN THE SALZKAMMERGUT
KING LUDWIG WAY

ITALY
ALTA VIA - High Level Walkis in the Dolomites
VIA FERRATA - Scrambles in the Dolomites
ITALIAN ROCK - Selected Rock Climbs in
 Northern Italy
CLASSIC CLIMBS IN THE DOLOMITES

OTHER AREAS
THE MOUNTAINS OF GREECE - A Walker's
Guide
CRETE: Off the beaten track
Treks & Climbs in the mountains of RHUM &
PETRA, JORDAN
THE ATLAS MOUNTAINS

GENERAL OUTDOOR BOOKS
LANDSCAPE PHOTOGRAPHY
FIRST AID FOR HILLWALKERS
MOUNTAIN WEATHER
MOUNTAINEERING LITERATURE
SKI THE NORDIC WAY
THE ADVENTURE ALTERNATIVE

CANOEING
SNOWDONIA WILD WATER, SEA & SURF
WILDWATER CANOEING
CANOEIST'S GUIDE TO THE NORTH EAST

CARTOON BOOKS
ON FOOT & FINGER
ON MORE FEET & FINGERS
LAUGHS ALONG THE PENNINE WAY

---

*Also a full range of guidebooks
to walking, scrambling, ice-climbing,
rock climbing, and other adventurous
pursuits in Britain and abroad*

---

*Other guides are constantly being added to the Cicerone List.
Available from bookshops, outdoor equipment shops or direct (send for price list)
from CICERONE, 2 POLICE SQUARE, MILNTHORPE, CUMBRIA, LA7 7PY*

CICERONE GUIDES

Cicerone publish a wide range of reliable guides to walking and climbing in
Britain - and other general interest books

LAKE DISTRICT - General Books
LAKELAND VILLAGES
WORDSWORTH'S DUDDON REVISITED
THE REGATTA MEN
REFLECTIONS ON THE LAKES
OUR CUMBRIA
PETTIE
THE HIGH FELLS OF LAKELAND
CONISTON COPPER A History
LAKELAND - A taste to remember (Recipes)
THE LOST RESORT?
CHRONICLES OF MILNTHORPE
LOST LANCASHIRE

LAKE DISTRICT - Guide Books
CASTLES IN CUMBRIA
WESTMORLAND HERITAGE WALK
IN SEARCH OF WESTMORLAND
CONISTON COPPER MINES
SCRAMBLES IN THE LAKE DISTRICT
MORE SCRAMBLES IN THE LAKE DISTRICT
WINTER CLIMBS IN THE LAKE DISTRICT
WALKS IN SILVERDALE/ARNSIDE
BIRDS OF MORECAMBE BAY
THE EDEN WAY

NORTHERN ENGLAND (outside the Lakes
THE YORKSHIRE DALES A walker's guide
WALKING IN THE SOUTH PENNINES
LAUGHS ALONG THE PENNINE WAY
WALKS IN THE YORKSHIRE DALES (3 VOL)
WALKS TO YORKSHIRE WATERFALLS
NORTH YORK MOORS Walks
THE CLEVELAND WAY & MISSING LINK
DOUGLAS VALLEY WAY
THE RIBBLE WAY
WALKING NORTHERN RAILWAYS EAST
WALKING NORTHERN RAILWAYS WEST
HERITAGE TRAILS IN NW ENGLAND
BIRDWATCHING ON MERSEYSIDE
THE LANCASTER CANAL
FIELD EXCURSIONS IN NW ENGLAND
ROCK CLIMBS LANCASHIRE & NW
THE ISLE OF MAN COASTAL PATH

DERBYSHIRE & EAST MIDLANDS
WHITE PEAK WALKS - 2 Vols
HIGH PEAK WALKS
WHITE PEAK WAY
KINDER LOG
THE VIKING WAY
THE DEVIL'S MILL (Novel)
WHISTLING CLOUGH (Novel)
WALES & WEST MIDLANDS
THE RIDGES OF SNOWDONIA
HILLWALKING IN SNOWDONIA
ASCENT OF SNOWDON
WELSH WINTER CLIMBS
SNOWDONIA WHITE WATER SEA & SURF
SCRAMBLES IN SNOWDONIA
ROCK CLIMBS IN WEST MIDLANDS
THE SHROPSHIRE HILLS A Walker's Guide

SOUTH & SOUTH WEST ENGLAND
WALKS IN KENT
THE WEALDWAY & VANGUARD WAY
SOUTH DOWNS WAY & DOWNS LINK
COTSWOLD WAY
WALKING ON DARTMOOR
SOUTH WEST WAY - 2 Vol

SCOTLAND
SCRAMBLES IN LOCHABER
SCRAMBLES IN SKYE
THE ISLAND OF RHUM
CAIRNGORMS WINTER CLIMBS
WINTER CLIMBS BEN NEVIS & GLENCOE
SCOTTISH RAILWAY WALKS
TORRIDON A Walker's Guide
SKI TOURING IN SCOTLAND

THE MOUNTAINS OF ENGLAND & WALES
VOL 1 WALES
VOL 2 ENGLAND

*Also a full range of guidebooks
to walking, scrambling, ice-climbing,
rock climbing, and other adventurous
pursuits in Europe*

*Other guides are constantly being added to the Cicerone List.
Available from bookshops, outdoor equipment shops or direct (send for price list)
from CICERONE, 2 POLICE SQUARE, MILNTHORPE, CUMBRIA, LA7 7PY*